Confessions
of a Non-Barbie

A Real Girl's Guide to Finding Beauty
and Pursuing Happily Ever-After

---

by
Kinda Wilson

*Jessica !
Hope you enjoy this !
Dream Big !
Eat lots of chocolate
Kinda
Wilson*

Harrison House
Tulsa, Oklahoma

15 14 13 12 11 10   10 9 8 7 6 5 4 3 2 1

Confessions of a Non-Barbie
A Real Girl's Guide to Finding Beauty and Pursuing Happily Ever-After
ISBN 13: 978-1-60683-008-6
Copyright © 2009 by Kinda Wilson
2950 E 76th Pl
Tulsa, OK 74136
Email: info@kindawilson.com

Published by Harrison House LLC
P.O. Box 35035
Tulsa, OK 74153
www.harrisonhouse.com

 Thanks

Thanks to so many friends who have listened to me talk endlessly about this project. Amy, Heidi, Josh, Garrett, Rachel, Cindy—your patience and friendship are more than I could ask for. Many thanks to all of the people who gave me plenty of material to write about and the teens and post-teens who gave me input. And thanks Mom and Dad, for giving me a picture of what a relationship should look like.

To Bryan Dirks of Press Group—thanks for all of your design and book advice and for trying to reform my messy design style. And the crew at Harrison House—you guys are priceless. Julie, Chris, Christina—I cannot imagine a better team to work with. Thanks for giving me this incredible opportunity and for being your crazy selves. I appreciate you all!

Table of Contents

Dating

Breakups - the Real Deal

Moving On...Eventually

Final Thoughts

About the Author

Endnotes

Endorsements

"Confessions of a non-Barbie is spiritual, wickedly sarcastic in all the right ways, and deep. Quite possibly one of the most exciting and fresh authors I've encountered in a long time."

--T. Suzanne Eller, Proverbs 31 Ministries
speaker and author of The Woman I Am Becoming

"This book kept me laughing at the realities of being a single girl. Raw and truthful, Kinda opens up her life and shares all the funny things we girls go through in our relationships, emotions and thoughts. I almost read the whole book in one sitting! Whether you are single, have single friends, or are a mom with a single daughter, this book will give you an amazing look into the funny and real-life moments of a single girl."

--Kristian Kelly, producer of skunkstv and speaker

"I loved Kinda's hilariously real depiction of the single girl—I immediately identified with the up and downs of her adventures. This book accurately describes the inner workings of a single girl—her hopes, dreams, emotions and feelings. It would help anyone be able to understand and identify with a single girl of any age!"

"So many girls and women will identify with this book."

--Cynthia McGuire, Young Single Women's Pastor,
Victory Christian Center, Tulsa

Introduction:

I'm not sure how this whole writing project got started, really. It feels like I just sort of woke up one day and found myself in the middle of it.

If I look back, I think I can trace its beginnings to high school with all of my journals filled with girly ballads and angry Alanis Morissette-inspired poetry. Happiness, bitterness, I felt it tangibly and overwhelmingly, and I wrote it all down.

Somewhere around college I hit even rougher emotions, and this time my journal entries changed slightly. I started writing down all of the things I had learned—had finally figured out—and the things I still struggled with. The things I wished someone had told me. The real, raw, in-your-face kind of things that stung like hydrogen peroxide on an open wound and the funny, ridiculous things that helped to heal and soothe it.

And I made lists about everything I had learned—fancy numbered lists with sub-headings and indented categories. I remember saying that girls need to know this stuff—the real stuff—and that someone should tell them. And I remember announcing it loudly and melodramatically to my friends and telling them how it would change the world.

And then, somewhere about there, I was writing a book. I wrote down all of the emotions I faced and all of the advice that had helped me. I documented all of the things I thought would help someone else. I wanted to pass along my insight about beauty and dating and guys and God. The ups, the downs, the all of it.

And here we are now with the completed project. I hope you enjoy it. More than that though, I hope it helps you see things a little differently than you did before. As you read this, may you realize that you are not alone in the crazy situations and emotions that you face. And may this book give you a bit of preparation for the situations you haven't yet encountered.

May you laugh at and learn from my embarrassing moments and find strength through what I've discovered. I am honored to have you read this—enjoy!

My cat is allergic
to velcro

Being single is
NOT a disease

I'm tired of "dating
Jesus"...and I think
the feeling is mutual!

Being a
Single Girl
—Emotions and
All!

Watch out for the
chick flicks

God says I'm beautiful, but
today I'm just not feelin' it!

12

Being single is not a disease - but people still try to "cure" you!

sin•gle [1] - [sing-guhl]
-adjective. 1. pertaining to the unmarried state: the single life
-noun. 2. one person or thing, a single one.

dis•ease [2] - [di-zeez] - noun.

1. A pathological condition of a part, organ, or system of an organism resulting from various causes...

2. A condition or tendency, as of society, regarded as abnormal and harmful.

Single. Just that word brings up a thousand thoughts and stories in my mind. (For one thing, it rhymes with Pringles, which are yummy with french onion dip. But that's a bit off-subject and not really helpful here).

I'm single you know, and I think I've heard it all–every statistic, everyone's advice, and everyone's deep word of wisdom for me. After a while, I guess I just had to figure out my own opinion. But good grief, have I gathered some interesting stories and viewpoints along the way. And I have a bad habit of sharing entirely too much information. Take last Sunday, for instance...

There I was, sitting in church, blissfully waiting for the sermon to begin. I had just finished singing, taken my customary drink at the water fountain, and made my way back to my seat. The visiting minister walked behind the podium and adjusted his microphone, tapping it to see if it was on. He noticed me as I took my seat in the second row. "Hey Kinda," he called out, "I haven't seen you in a while.

Do you have a boyfriend yet?" Well, apparently his microphone was working fine now! The entire church turned to look at me. But wait, he wasn't finished yet. "Because if you don't have one, I could help you out with that!" And if that wasn't bad enough, most of the church broke out in applause. It was like the whole world was trying to help me overcome my singleness.

Now I don't think being single is that bad—it has its ups and downs. But people have the oddest reactions when they hear that I'm single and there's no way for me to talk about boys and dating without first looking at how I and others view my single-girl status. Let me give you a brief glimpse of some of the responses I get:

- Oh honey, I'm sorry
- What's the matter, can't you find you a man yet?
- So why did you decide not to get married?
- What was wrong with that last guy you dated…what was his name again?
- You know you only have _____ years left to have children; how does your mother feel about that?
- (Kind look of sympathy)

I just smile and tell them I'm waiting for the *right* guy, but after a while it gets a little old.

When my great Aunt Bertha* pinches my cheeks for the twentieth time and asks what's wrong with me because I can't get a man, I have to admit I have a few evil thoughts running through my head. I tell her I'm waiting for God's timing, but my eyes sparkle with amusement as I think about what I'd *really* like to tell her:

- Yeah, let me put an order in for one of those—what's that address for Dell's customize-a-man website?
- Find a man? Ohhhh, phew, I thought I had to be more specific than that. Hold on a second, let me Google "desperate man."
- Ooooh—*find* a man. All these years I thought they were saying *frying pan*—so that's what I've been doing wrong!

* = Name changed to protect the not-so-innocent

Thankfully, Aunt Bertha will never know what I've been thinking and I can keep getting those socks for Christmas. But why do they all want me married so quickly? Do they think that I'm intentionally trying to not find the right guy—that I'm running out of time? What's wrong with being single? Maybe my biological clock is a giant grandfather clock that ticks and tocks and sets off a huge cuckoo bird alarm every hour or two. Maybe they think I'm so miserable that they need to rescue me by setting me up with their great second cousin-in-law. Or maybe, just maybe, they only want me to be happy and they're trying to help out in the only way they know.

15

I decided to take their helpful advice a while back, and I finally gave in when my friend insisted that I go out with one of her guy-friends on the dreaded "blind date". Now I'm not opposed to meeting new people of the opposite sex, and I'm definitely not opposed to dating. There's just something about blind dates that screams, "Here God, please play a practical joke on me," but I hadn't been on a blind date before, so I thought I would give it a try.

The date started off well enough—I was impressed when he picked a nice restaurant and encouraged me to order what I wanted. I was less impressed later when he chased down the waitress to split our ticket (so I could pay for my half). It was then and there that I decided being single wasn't so bad. I decided that I would like to be in a relationship with the right guy someday, but until he came along, I would still enjoy my life as a single girl.

The official receipt ⟶

Our culture likes to argue this point with me sometimes. Society seems to scream that guys are the end prize and only prize in the game of life. That the girls who have found men are winners (no matter how dysfunctional their relationships are), and the girls who have not successfully found a man are lacking, unlucky, or still waiting around to find one.

16 My View

I have news for you, "getting a man" is great, but it's not the end-all, be-all, Nobel-Oscar-Emmy Prize in the game of life. Relationships can be fulfilling, but if you're stacking all your happiness bets on the "find a husband" card, you might end up disappointed in the outcome. A man will not solve all of your problems, fix all of your childhood issues, or bring back your dog Fluffy that disappeared when you were eight. A man will not be the magic purpose in life that you've been searching for. And for those of you waiting until you find a man to live life, that may not be the best strategy to get you a man anyway. Most men are attracted to women who have other hobbies, interests, and goals in their lives besides them.

So the way I see it, you have three choices as a single girl:

1. Get with the wrong guy, because he's the one who's there and all of your friends are dating
2. Be miserable waiting for the right guy
3. Be an interesting, productive person waiting for the right guy

Number three sounds like a winner to me. So make good use of your time as a single girl. It's okay to be single, and you shouldn't put your life on hold waiting until your Prince Charming comes along.

Sometimes it's easy to use the line, "When I get a man, I'm going to go to such-and-such restaurant," or, "When I get a boyfriend, I'm going to go here, do this, enjoy this, etc." Granted, some things are better when enjoyed with a significant other. A candle-lit dinner just isn't the same by yourself. But there's no reason why you should avoid every restaurant, beautiful scenic view, romantic setting, vacation trip, and sporting event just because you're single.

Live it up—enjoy life. I have come to the conclusion that I'm seeing as many sights as I can while I'm single, and then when I find my guy, I'll know which places I want to take him back to. It doesn't mean that I'm not still looking for a guy; it just means I'm enjoying the trip to find him.

So don't let anyone get you down or convince you that you're living a substandard life until your man comes along. You might get lonely, down, or discouraged along the way—you might even really wish that you had a date—but that doesn't mean that you can't have a heck of a life as a single girl until you find your dreamboat.

17

As for all of those "helpful" people? Well, keep in mind that they have your best interest at heart, and they just want to see you happy. And be nice to Aunt Bertha, she just wants grandchildren of her own.

Things I've Learned: Enjoy your life as a single girl—Make the most of it.

This Space For Writing Messages

POST CARD

Place Stamp Here
Domestic One cent
Foreign Two cents

If you create a life that is full of things you enjoy and love, if you find new interests and take joy in discovering new things, you will find that you have a full life and are a person that attracts interest.

Confidential

Some extra wisdom from

a girl who's been there

—*Misty,* 32

This side for the Address only

It may be a while before I find someone
To take me to the football games
To buy me a hotdog
When I think they're too expensive
So I'll buy my tickets in advance
I'll save my pennies now
It may be a while before I find someone
Who does the handy work
Helps me out and carries boxes
I'll roll my sleeves up, get my hands dirty
I'll refuse to be helpless
It may be a while before I find someone
Who loves me more than life
Who understands and likes me when
My mood is "complicated"
It's true. It might be a while.
It might take some time to find him
And so I can't take chances now
And put my life on hold
I'll love myself in spite of things
I'll not back down on life
I'll do the things I've held in dream
I'll make my wishes true
So in case he takes a while to show up
I'll still enjoy the view

I'm tired of "dating Jesus"...and I think the feeling is mutual

As fun as it is being a single girl and as much as I enjoy my freedom, there are times when I just get tired of being on my own. I have been to singles' groups and heard sooo many single (and married) women give pep talks and tell their stories that I think I have them memorized. I have appreciated them, but after a while, I get tired of hearing how much I should love "dating Jesus," and I just want to spend a Friday evening with a guy who thinks I'm special.

Don't get me wrong, the most important thing is to find out who you are in God before you go looking for a guy. You will not be able to have the most fulfilling relationship with a man without developing your relationship with God first.

But I've gotta tell you a little secret. (I'm saying this in a hushed tone so other uptight people won't hear it and freak out) "Dating Jesus" is fine and all, but sometimes I just want a real date.

After all, who's going to take me to a New Year's Eve party? Is Jesus going to show up with a corsage? I'm going to look pretty silly going to dinner with a chair reserved for Jesus. Come on God, help a sista out!

And to tell you the truth, I think Jesus is on my side for this one. I think if He has to listen to me another Friday night, He's going to personally put my profile on match.com for me.

I can picture Him now...

Jesus: About that Kinda girl, don't You think it's time she had a date?

God: It's not time for her yet; there are still things she needs to do.

Jesus: I know, I know, but did You hear her last Friday night? She wrote four songs and seven poems.

God: She's still depending on You, she's doing okay—it's good for her.

20 Jesus: Maybe, but I had to listen to all of the songs—and she can barely even play that guitar. It's wearing Me out; I think maybe We should help her out a bit.....hmmmm........You know I could put a pic up on match.com for her and she'd never know it was Me.....

That's how I view the situation. Being single is wonderful. It lets you focus on you and what you want to accomplish in life. But there are times when being single just plain stinks. When you get an invitation to a party or wedding and you don't have an "And Guest." When your good friends are getting roses delivered to their doors. When your car breaks down and you're stranded at the side of the road. Those are the times where you think, *You know, it would be really nice just to have someone to lean on right now. It would be really nice to have someone to*

handle the situation and let me rest for a while. Even the most independent girls will admit that they would like to have someone to help them carry their bags or to take them to dinner. And even the holiest Christian girls get lonely sometimes. That's right, I said it. You just get lonely for a boyfriend sometimes.

We all look brave and strong, put our game faces on, and strut around like we don't care who pays attention to us. Then we lie awake at night, staring at the ceiling, thinking about what it would be like to have someone who thinks we are wonderful. We just want someone to stick up for us, support us, encourage us, and make us feel special.

21

But you know what, when I don't have that and the guy isn't available, God is still there. He comforts me when I cry, He listens to me babble and blubber about what I think I need and how frustrated I am. He sends a special blessing my way to cheer me up when no one else even knows that I'm down. So I guess until a real date comes my way, I'll be thankful for what I have and keep enjoying my time as a single girl.

Things I've Learned: Being a single girl gets lonely sometimes, but God helps out.

Watch out for the chick flicks

Lorri was always one of those good friends. The real kind. We used to stay up half of the night lamenting about boys and giggling about nothing in particular. About three or four in the morning, we would get giddy and a bit loopy, and pretty much anything was funny after that. She threw a blanket over her head once and just sat on my living room floor, pretending she was a tent, I think. You don't find friends like that very often.

Lorri as a tent

After she moved away, I missed the late-night talks that we used to have. We still kept in touch, but it was more of a monthly catch-up talk rather our usual heart-to-hearts. A while ago, she flew back in to visit and stayed with me for the week. I gladly loaned her my couch and it felt like old times again. I had my friend Lorri back, and we filled the week with chick flicks and girl talk.

When she left to go back home, she left me an interesting surprise present. She wrote notes on small pieces of paper and hid them all around my house. It took me almost a year to find them all (I don't clean my room very often).

I still have one of the notes that she left for me under the VCR. It said:

Don't watch too many chick flicks - we know what that does!

-- Lorri

The note was funny, but it had a serious bit of truth to it. Some of my guy friends looked at the note and didn't get it, but all of the girls did.

Every girl can tell you what happens when you watch a chick flick. You get caught up in the movie, the story, the fantasy. You become the lead actress, and you win the guy. All of your dreams come to life on the big screen and (if it's a good chick flick) you're totally swept away.

23

I knew exactly what Lorri's note was talking about. Watching a chick flick is fine, but there are times when you do *not* need to be caught up in the fantasy world of girls, guys, and love triangles. If you're already vulnerable when you start watching those movies, it's easy to get into an emotional fantasy tailspin. Sometimes you need to guard your heart against something that may be innocent but will take your mind and emotions to places that will be distracting or depressing.

And it goes beyond just being careful about chick flicks. You *really* have to watch out for the "romantic occasions" such as dances, weddings, or even Valentine's Day. Wow, do those occasions ever bring out the "I-wish-I-had-a-man" feelings. I can be completely content being a single girl, and then the 14th of February starts getting close. I don't know what it is about giant pink gorillas holding hearts that sets me off, but I kind of want to take the ugly things and chunk them in the river. And I'm not bitter, I promise! My system just hits sappy overload in February.

For the situations that you cannot avoid, try to make the best of them so you won't feel down in the dumps. Find a way to still enjoy those occasions that

The giant gorilla

would normally be reserved for romantic couples. Have a girls' night out on Valentine's Day and treat yourselves to something special. I usually buy something for my single girlfriends on Valentine's Day, just to let them know how much they mean to me.

As for the situations that you *can* avoid? Don't volunteer yourself for an emotionally painful day if you don't have to. Guard your heart—be careful about what thoughts and ideas you let play over and over in your mind.

24

Above all else, guard your heart, for it is the wellspring of life.

Proverbs 4:23 NIV

Maybe you shouldn't listen to that depressing song about how the girl never found true love. If you've had that sad song on "repeat" for so long that your CD is starting to skip, maybe you should try listening to something with at least a bit of hope instead. And maybe you and I both should take Lorri's advice and watch out for those chick flicks!

Things I've Learned: Find out what triggers your lonely feelings. If it's a cheesy soap opera— stay away!

Maybe I should have opened the can first

"You looked fantastic today!" I looked at the text message again, although I don't know why. I had it memorized. I had been staring at it off and on for the past hour. My friend smirked at the dopey look on my face, but I just rolled my eyes—briefly of course—and then gazed back at the screen. As if me looking at it would

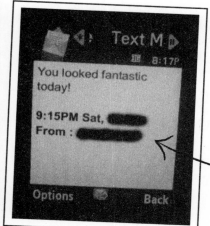

make more words appear—perhaps describing my eyes or hair and comparing my beauty to various goddesses. I thought maybe, just maybe, the entire Song of Solomon would appear in my inbox if I checked my messages again. I sighed. He thought I looked fantastic.

You don't need to know that

It's strange how that message meant more to me than countless friends and relatives telling me that I was special. This was different. It was a message *from a guy*. Telling me I looked *fantastic*. It meant I might be a girl people found attractive. And as much as I hated to admit it, that thought was very important to me.

I've always considered myself pretty average looking. About a six-point-five out of ten I would say. I didn't look too bad all spiffied up and all, but the rest of the time I was just so-so. I liked my eyes but not-so-much my nose. My hips and waist were okay, but my legs? Well, the world didn't need to see those. So when a guy sent a text message about my looks, it made me all giggly inside.

Maybe beauty's a sore spot for me. As a single girl, I tend to question how I look every time a guy looks (or doesn't look) my way. The way I look is the first thing I blame when I get rejected and the one thing that still stings a little if people harass me about it. I sometimes get so caught up in all of the frenzy to be "hot" that I compare how I look to the girls around me to see if I measure up, to see if I can "beat the competition."

Yet if someone asks me what beauty is, it's hard for me to explain. I'm not one-hundred percent sure how to describe it, and I haven't figured out an exact formula yet for how to get it. I just know that whatever true beauty is, I want to have or be it. The minute I was old enough to be aware of my surroundings, the world started telling me how important it was to be beautiful. I can remember comments as far back as early elementary school—kids saying that someone was ugly or pretty—and kids can be ruthless.

Since then the messages haven't disappeared, they've only become more refined. Every time I turn on the TV or read a magazine I'm told at least three things about beauty:

1. I must have beauty to get a man.
2. Beauty is long legs, a tiny waist, and big boobs.
3. Beauty is whatever brand of nail polish they're selling.

That's all beauty is? It's just not true. It can't be. If I believe the image of the stick-thin girl with long blond hair is the only way to be attractive, then I'm selling guys way too short. Yeah, there are some shallow guys out there, but they're not all looking for a Barbie clone, I promise. Guys are attracted to different "looks" and "types" of girls. I forget this sometimes and get swayed by images that I see around me. I start thinking that every guy only wants a blond "36-24-36", and I compare myself to that. Well, I look horrible as a blond, and the only "36-24-36" I'm ever going to have is a locker combination. I have to remind myself that some guys are more attracted to brunettes or redheads, and some guys just don't care about hair color at all. After all, my girl friends and I are attracted to different guys (thank goodness), so why is it so hard for me to believe that guys are attracted to different girls?

Beyond just hair color and waist size, how a girl carries herself can make her look like a million bucks. The way a girl acts can add or take away from her beauty just as much (if not more) than the shape of her nose or the arch of her eyebrow.

27

Yes, attraction is important in a relationship, but I think beauty is more like

a label on a can, to use one of my weird analogies. The labels on the food containers catch your eye if you find them interesting. They cause you to stop, look at the food, and think about buying it. However, if the food tastes really bad or is rotten, it doesn't matter how good the label looks, you aren't going to be a repeat customer.

Isn't that kind of how beauty is? Most of us have a feature or certain "look" that we're initially attracted to. If we walk into a room and see a guy who resembles what we think is our "type," we stop,

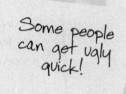

Some people can get ugly quick!

give him a second look, and maybe go over and talk to him. But people seem to get more or less cute the more you hang around them. Trust me, some people can get ugly quick!

I have met some hot guys that were self-absorbed jerks. After a short conversation with them, they suddenly didn't seem so cute anymore. It was like they had a cute label on the outside but were rotten on the inside. Nope—I didn't want any more of that, thank you very much. And some guys that I didn't notice at first suddenly got *very* attractive after I found out how cool they were.

So what can I learn from all of this? I know that if I'm "rotten," it doesn't matter how much hair gel I use or how many pair of expensive shoes I buy, I will still be a pain in the neck to hang out with. On the flip side, if I focus on enjoying life and doing things that I love, it will only make me more attractive. Being my crazy unique self enjoying life is what makes me beautiful. It isn't only one or two superficial traits, but beauty is the whole of who I am, the essence of what makes me tick, and the passion that makes my eyes sparkle. Yep, that's what makes beauty harder to define, but that's what makes it beauty.

And what about those guys who *are* only looking for Barbie clones? Well, if a guy is so caught up in a certain hair color or chest size that he doesn't notice me, it's his loss. I'm movin' on. It's good to know that I didn't waste my time on a superficial punk, and I didn't want a shallow guy anyway. I'll just wait for the guy who's looking for real beauty.

28

Things I've Learned: Beauty is more than just a waist size.

A guy's perspective

Things that make a girl beautiful:

By: Stephen C.
a) confidence
b) intelligence
c) playfulness

By Ron S.
d) it's all in the smile
e) brains
f) self-respect

Tips to be Beautiful

- Find something you love to do and do it.

There is something so attractive about a girl who has found something in life that she loves to do (besides looking at guys).

- Be comfortable in your own skin. Just like yourself.

Confidence is *very* attractive. Now, I didn't say fall in love with a mirror and obsess over your looks. I said just be comfortable being you. I'll bet most guys don't even notice all of those tiny "flaws" that you obsess over. One of my good friends keeps complaining about how her nose is crooked. I never noticed until she pointed it out – over and over.

30

God,
I don't feel pretty today
I don't think I even feel plain
I know I'm not substandard, surely,
But I feel rejected all the same
I realize I'm in a different category
Perhaps a different league
But sometimes I feel they changed the sport
And someone forgot to tell me
So all the players run for downs
And me stuck with my glove
I'm all alone in far left field
Playing a game of one

God says I'm beautiful, but today I'm just not feelin' it!

This morning I got up on the wrong side of something and never quite figured out how to get back. I finally rolled out of bed, stumbled to the bathroom mirror, and sighed. My nose was all puffy, my hair was sticking out five-thousand different directions, and my skin looked blotchy. This was going to be one of those days: an "ugly" day.

I wanted to hide in my room in my comfy pajamas with a baseball cap covering any trace of who I was. I just didn't feel up to facing the world - not looking like this.

I knew down deep inside that I was an okay-looking girl. I knew that somewhere out there some guy probably thought I was attractive. I knew that in God I had a purpose, and I was a talented, intelligent woman.

...And yet I felt ugly. I can't explain why, I just felt crummy, "unpretty," and definitely unlovely.

As much as I can intellectualize it and say that I know what beauty is or that it comes from the inside out, once in a while my human emotions come through. Even though I am okay with who I am, and even though I know that God created me to be a beautiful woman, I still have what I like to call "ugly" days. Sometimes they're triggered by what goes on around me. I can be absolutely fine and happy with life. Then one guy will make a comment to me about how beautiful another girl is—one girl will make a crack about one of my features—and I catch my breath. A small part of me hesitates and wonders, *I am okay....aren't I?*

Then again, sometimes an ugly day can be triggered by absolutely nothing at all. I get up in the morning and *wham*—I feel blahhh. All of those nice little (true) beliefs about being beautiful in God just fly right out the window. I look in the mirror and wonder, *Am I pretty enough? Am I good enough? Look at my nose and figure—am I a beautiful treasure that someone will actually want?* I'm not sure I measure up to that "beautiful lover" spoken about in the Song of Solomon:

32

> *Your lips are like a scarlet ribbon; your mouth is lovely. Your temples behind your veil are like the halves of a pomegranate.*
>
> Song of Solomon 4:3 NIV

Some days, like today for me, I'm just not there. I'm not jiving with the whole "I'm the beautiful lover whose lips are like a scarlet ribbon" bit. I think I'm closer to "I'm an average, grouchy girl with PMS." Somehow that doesn't fit quite as well into the Song of Solomon now does it?

> *Oh average, grouchy girl with PMS, your lips are a bit chapped from the windy weather. Your temples have a bit of acne and could use a tan. Oh, how I love thee average, grouchy girl. (Verse: never gonna happen)*

So if I know that God made me beautiful, but I don't feel beautiful today, what does that mean? Shouldn't I feel pretty and peppy and positive?

Here's the truth of the situation: *Knowing* that I am beautiful in God doesn't mean that I won't *feel* bland, plain, or even ugly sometimes. Everyone, and I mean everyone, has down times.

I have times that I just don't feel like I'm anything special. Times when I'd give anything to trade out my nose, lips, or figure with some more fortunate pic-ture-perfect girl. That does not mean that I'm not special. It doesn't make the *truth* about my beauty any less true. It simply means that I'm still human and I have to deal with normal emotions.

The _truth_ about beauty:
- Beauty is not just a waist or butt size
- Guys are attracted to all kinds of "types" and "looks"
- A girl's confidence and smile can be very attractive to a guy
- What makes you beautiful is _you_—the whole of you, the essence of you—what you love to do, and what you are
- You are definitely beautiful!

33

Emotions that you may deal with anyway:
- Feeling plain
- Ugly
- Inferior
- Unloveable
- Not good enough
- Out of place
- Anything but special
- Like no one understands

First of all, remember that it's normal to have these emotions—I'm there with you. People who look like their lives have always been perfect and they've always had it together? They haven't. Those beautiful girls who look like they should be on the front of a swimsuit calendar? They have ugly days too, and they don't always feel like the gorgeous people you think they are.

Beauty – What men chase after. What novels are based on and girls dream about. What God has created within each one of us.

Ugly – How I feel when I look in the mirror in the morning. How I feel when I'm left out. How I feel for no reason at all sometimes.

To overcome those ugly emotions, you have to act from what you know is true about your beauty and not from what you feel. Get God's opinion about your beauty. Discover the characteristics that make you unique and priceless. Keep reminding yourself that emotions do not equal truth, and that it's okay to feel a little sub-par. It doesn't mean that you're not a smokin' hot chica.

34

So let your crazy self shine through. Walk like you own the world, because you do. Don't let a comment or a crummy day sidetrack you from knowing at your core that you are something magnificent. And make sure you hang around people who support you and yo' beautiful self—not people who compete against you and try to tear you down.

Things I've Learned: You are beautiful, even if you don't always feel like it.

For you created my inmost being; you knit me together in my mother's womb. I praise you because I am fearfully and wonderfully made; your works are wonderful, I know that full well.

Psalm 139: 13-14 NIV

Looking for Beauty

For a second
I looked in the mirror
And I was beautiful
The lovely princess
Waiting to be rescued
By some handsome knight
Of my dreams
Beauty that angels envied
And men dreamed of
And everyone wanted to know me
The real me
And most of all
They wanted me
I belonged
And then I looked again
And I was still me
Plain
No following crowd
Haunting no one's dreams
And I was still alone
And lonely

Reminder to self...I am
beautiful anyway, so read
this again

If our friendship were a movie, it would be a drama

They say we tend to become like the most important people in our lives think we will become.

It's that look, you know? That look someone gives you that says you're not quite cool. The smirk and half-raised eyebrow that seems to stretch off the person's forehead and slap you in the face. Although it would be amusing to see an eyebrow slap someone, it doesn't feel quite as funny at the time. In fact, I don't think there are many worse feelings in the world than having someone look at you like you're an idiot. Except maybe the feeling you get when someone says things about you behind your back. It's even worse when that other person is your friend—a person who is close to you.

It's amazing how much of an effect our friends can have on us and our images as single girls. Just one look can make us question ourselves, our beauty, and our worth. Just one comment can make us wonder if we are pretty enough or cool enough to fit in with the crowd or find a man. And it seems like some people just make it their mission to bring negativity to the world and make life miserable. Those people can make me feel like nothing I ever do is right. I know, you can picture one of those people in your mind right now, right?

The funny thing is, I have hung out with some of those negative people anyway, even when I didn't want to. I have even called them friends and confided ʰem about my problems. Why did I do that? Was it because I didn't want to ᵉlings? Were they my safe comfort zone? Whatever the case, I have

ᵈ the value of true friendships and the beauty of supportive gured out that I can *choose* who I want to hang around and be influenced by. Now I'm not talking about the people who are acquaintances who I rarely see. I can be friendly and polite to everyone, but I need to carefully consider who I want to bring in to my close circle of friends.

Why? We tend to be influenced by close friends, whether we realize it or not. We also start to become more like our inner circle of friends, and we sometimes start acting like who *they* think we are.

I have noticed that if my friends give me words of encouragement and treat me like a beautiful woman, then after a while I start to feel like a queen. However, certain people I have hung around (no, I'm not naming names) have always made small critical remarks and given me looks that made me question myself. After hanging out with them for a while, I wanted to crawl under a rock. And not a cute "pet rock" either—an ugly grimy, moss-covered rock. Not a good positive reinforcement for my beauty.

So although you can have many friends and mentor many types of people, be careful who you spend your close personal time with and who you seek advice from. If your "friends" keep tearing you down or making cracks about your appearance, watch out.

Warning signs that your "friends" may not be good for you:

- You always seem to feel down, dejected, or tired after hanging out with them.
- You have to constantly be on your guard around them to protect yourself.
- They make "jokes" about your looks (especially around guys) to make themselves look cooler.
- Their "critiquing" of you is not done in a loving, constructive way.
- Their "cracks" about you are aimed more at hurting you than mutual joking around.
- They seem to be in your life because of the benefits they get from your friendship.

Be careful about letting these people in as your close, intimate friends. After a while those little comments start taking a toll on who you are and what you believe about yourself. Your friends should make you feel like you're the most beautiful girl in the world.

Proactively seek out friends and mentors who are like who you want to be. It's a good idea to find people you admire (who have qualities that you respect, etc) and see if they would like to hang out some time. It may seem a little strange and even scary at first to seek out new friends. You may feel funny asking people to be your friend and spend time with you. You may even be worried about the reaction you will get from some of your not-so-supportive friends. It will be worth it though—you need people in your life who will be true friends. Find people who build you up instead of tearing you down and making you feel "unbeautiful" and unwanted.

38

Things I've Learned: Hang out with the girls who make you feel beautiful, not the ones who act like there's something wrong with you.

Straight through the cracks
Current mood: let down

I'm a strong woman, I have no problem
Keeping my head up high
You've seen me be stable,
You've brought me your problems
I've held the whole world while it cried
But nobody noticed that I was only smiling
Through my lips but not my eyes
Nobody asked me if I could do better
And so they passed me by

And I slipped straight through the cracks
Of every friendship and every whim
And I fell beneath the burden
Of every worry and every sin
And you never noticed that I was getting tired
Of forever carrying you
You were too busy crying to look at my shoulder
And wonder if I needed help too

I've always been wise for a woman of my years
And I've offered with no regret
You needed my help, I was so glad to give it
And so I gave till it hurt
But who do I look to when I hit a rough spot
And who's here to wipe away tears
And who does the holding when I need to crumble
Cause I've been crumbling for years

My cat is allergic to Velcro

What if finding someone to connect with is not possible? Sometimes you go through seasons when you just can't seem to find *any* supportive friends. It may be that the people in your life can't relate to the things that you are going through. Or it may be that circumstances such as moving or changing jobs have temporarily taken close friends out of your life. Or worst of all, it could be that the girls who should be helping you are actually part of the problem ("Jaws" theme music here).

You would think that as girls we would realize that we need to help each other out. But I think that some girls missed the memo about being all sisterly, supportive, and sympathetic. I remember in high school that the people who made fun of girls the most about their figures and weights were *other girls*. I have seen girls turn catty on each other so quickly it would make your head spin, all to win some bizarre social competition. They spread rumors, stabbed friends in the back, and called other girls names that would make my grandma gasp in horror. It was like watching a carnivore special on the Discovery Channel.

Whatever the reason, not having a friend close by to help out in a rough situation makes life seem even lonelier. If life were geometry, this season would be a cube. I like to picture it as a large cardboard-looking box, and you're stuck in it. A cardboard box with tall sides so that you can't see anything around you or any way out.

The box that you're in may be a town or community. Or your box could be a situation you're going through, a time-consuming job, or even high school. High school is sort of a world of its own, with its own rules and society. It's so all-consuming that it feels like what you see everyday is what the entire world is like. That's great if you have a cool group of friends to hang out with, and it's horrible if you're in a place with people who try to make your life miserable. The problem is, if you get stuck in a crummy high school environment, you can't exactly up and switch schools like you would the grocery store where you shop. You're stuck with dealing with the same people, over and over.

You feel trapped. Alone. Lonely. How frustrating! There's no one around for support and no one to cheer you up. You have a dream in your mind about where you want to go but you *can't see it anywhere*. You know there must be people somewhere who understand you and will support you but *you can't find them*. Yep, it's like you're stuck in a box.

41

It is during these "box" times that you must reach deep inside yourself to lift your spirits. It is during these times that you have to be a friend to yourself when you cannot find one. When no one else is there to be a cheerleader and to make you feel beautiful, you've gotta give yourself a pep talk. When no one else is there to give you encouragement, you've gotta look in the mirror and start preachin' like crazy. No one may be there at 3:00 in the morning when you wake up crying, so you've got to remind yourself of what you know is true. Remind yourself of what God thinks of you.

> *The LORD your God is with you, he is mighty to save. He will take great delight in you, he will quiet you with his love, he will rejoice over you with singing.*
>
> *Zephaniah 3:17 NIV.*

Does this feel as wonderful as having a friend give you words of support and encouragement? Maybe not, but sometimes you're all you've got, and you've *got* to step it up and support yourself. You're special and beautiful and you know it, even if no one else has told you lately. Even if you've somehow been overlooked all week, month, or even year. God Himself wants to remind you of how much you mean to Him. So go to His Word, talk to Him, and let Him remind you of how cool you are. Then look straight in the mirror, tears and all, and remind yourself that you're not backing down from life one bit.

Need some help getting started? Use what applies from this and give it a try:

" *All right, come on girl. No one's here but you, and you've got to get it together. You're worth it. If no one's here to support you, if no one understands you, you'll make it just fine. You can't slow down now. You're going through a bunch of (insert situation here), that's true, but that's okay. It doesn't matter what they said about you, they're crazy, and you're classier than that. Keep your head up. You are awesome. You are incredible. You've got plenty enough to make it on your own, and I think you're doing fine. God will help you out, you'll come out on top, and the whole world will wonder how they overlooked you. Just keep going, you can do it!* "

Not quite feeling it yet? Try it again, and this time with more "umph!" In fact, do more than just give yourself a pep talk, *write it down*. Declare it. Tape it on your wall. Cut it out in big velcro letters and stick it on your cat—whatever it takes. Then do something special for yourself. It may not get you dancing around the room in jubilation at first, but after a while it starts to sink in. After a while you start listening to what you're telling yourself and your spirit begins to lift.

Keep encouraging yourself when no one else is there. Know that you will not be in the place you are in right now forever. Situations, jobs, towns, schools—they all change eventually. Keep reminding yourself that what you're going through is a *season* and seasons change. The emotions that you are feeling are *temporary,* and the truth will show up in your life soon. Before you know it you'll be in a better situation and you'll have people who will support and appreciate you. Until then, keep your head up, don't give up, and keep walking it out.

43

Things I've Learned: Sometimes you gotta give yourself a pep talk to get through the tough times.

My personal pep talk
Current mood: stubborn

A letter to me
Because I'm cool
And I've come to like me a lot
Just wanted to let you know
In case
No one has told you lately
That I think you are holding up
And fighting still
Quite bravely
Just wanted to tell you
That you're all right
And others should be proud
To have the time to spend with you
To have you hang around....

Thinkin' about You (Yes, YOU)

You are NOT alone
It may feel like it
It may look like it
But it just isn't so
There are a thousand people who have
prayed for you
Hoped for you, cried for you
And a thousand more who are
waiting to meet you
You may not see it yet
But it will come
You are NOT alone
There is someone, even now
Who is praying for a friend,
For a kindred, for a smile
And they are wishing they could meet you
There is someone, even now
Who is praying for a lover,
For a soulmate, for a smile
And they are wishing they could know you
Do not get down just because you do not
see it
Yet
Do not give up because it's not within your
View

I've got you under my skin

I'm thinking of getting a tattoo. I know, I know, your momma would gasp and cover your eyes if she saw you reading this. But I think tattoos are interesting. You can tell a lot about a person by what they choose to permanently imprint on their body. I personally wouldn't want a tattoo if it didn't have meaning to me.

I've thought a lot about it, and I'm leaning toward having the word "blessed" printed in Hindi script on my ring finger. The word "blessed" because I never want to forget that I am truly blessed by God—even when I do not understand life. Even when I do not feel like I am blessed. Hindi because India was the first place I traveled overseas and realized exactly how truly fortunate I am.

Yep, if I ever choose to ingrain something on the fabric of my being, "blessed" is what it will be. I want it to sink through the fibers of my skin, circulate through my blood, and echo in the chambers of my mind. And yes, if I could, I would tattoo it on my mind as well.

After all, we all have something imprinted there anyway. Good, bad, self-serving, self-loathing; something is there. It may not be as initially visible as an inked-up sleeve, but it will surface eventually.

It's usually something someone has told us about ourselves that we have "taken to heart." We have taken it in, imprinted it on our minds, and told ourselves that's who we are. Even when the people who told us that disappear from our lives, we keep their sayings repeating in our heads like an old mouthy parrot with a short vocabulary.

We don't even realize these things are there half of the time, but they still show up. We will have an incredible idea, and something in the back of our minds will speak up: "Oh no, I couldn't do that. I'm just not smart/funny/popular enough."

And those thoughts influence who we are and what we do. They influence how beautiful we think we are and what we think we're worth. Those thoughts are tattoos.

I remember one boy in the eighth grade who continually called me chicken-legs. It was true—I was pretty scrawny. That phrase stayed with me for years in my mind, and I would repeat it whenever I wore anything that showed my legs at all. Then one of my teenage friends set me straight. "Kinda, I don't know what you looked like then, but your legs are fine now. They look normal to me. And that skirt looks cute on you." Then she basically told me to shut up and quit complaining—I needed that.

I hadn't realized what was tattooed on my mind. And that it wasn't true. This is a pretty mild example, but it made me think about the other things I was telling myself everyday.

You want to see something crazy? Take a journal with you and write down your random thoughts for an entire day. Then you'll see what you've been tattooing on your mind. It's good to look at—compare what you're thinking to what is true about you. What does God think about you? What is the truth? Then work on stopping all the negative junk you tell yourself every day.

As I mentioned before, be aware of who you surround yourself with and who you allow to speak into your life. Guard your heart. Be very careful about who you tell your dreams to and who you allow to affect your self-image.

Tattoo something good on your mind. Start by telling yourself that God has plans for you to succeed and prosper. Tell yourself you are a wonderful, talented creation, blessed by God. And it wouldn't hurt to start tattooing a few of your friends either...

Things I've Learned: You've gotta watch what gets imprinted on your mind.

My confession:

My friend Amy got tired of my complaining once and made me wear a "negativity-zapper" bracelet. The idea was to snap it against my wrist when I said/thought something completely negative about myself. Once I didn't even realize that I had said something negative about me, and she leaned over and snapped the fire out of my wrist. I don't know how much it helped, but it left red marks up and down my wrist. Apparently I'm still working on this whole "positive thought" thing.

I think I saw a sparkler...let's make out!

Girls are confusing - guys are oblivious

Apparently I'm triangle-shaped

Looking for a Date

I'm a 7-pound bass (in a vegetarian restaurant)

I always go for the bad boys...

THE TOP 5

CHEESY PICKUP LINES - USE AT YOUR OWN RISK!

1. There's something wrong with my cell phone...it doesn't have your number on it.

2. Do you have a band-aid? I scraped my knee falling for you.

3. You must be Jamaican cause Jamaican me craaaazy!

4. Are you from Tennessee? Cause you're the only ten I see!

5. Do you believe in the hereafter? Because I'm here after you!

Girls are confusing - guys are oblivious

I looked at Brian* from across the room as he ate his chocolate-chip cookie and sipped his Starbucks frappu-something-or-other. Wow, he was cute. He had that slightly-gelled, mussed-up hair look, and he walked around with just the right amount of confidence that seemed to say, "Yep, I *meant* for it to look this way." He was one of those Vans and blazer kind of guys, and it intrigued me. Oh, and did I mention that he didn't know that I existed? I mean *really* know that I existed. *Really* know—like stays up at night thinking about me and calls after a natural disaster to make sure that I'm safe. Nope, I was not even on his radar. We had talked a few times in passing over coffee and bagels, but I think our discussion about the packet of sugar was about as deep as it got. I watched as he walked by me. I wanted to trip him on his way out the door and yell, *"Hey look at me buddy"* as he was on his way down—before he hit the concrete, preferably.

I thought about the situation. He wasn't picking up on my "this is supposed to be a fairy-tale" vibe. Maybe my "viber" was broken or something. So now what was I supposed to do? Should I wait around for him to receive a neon vision of writing on a wall about me? Should I give him a not-so-subtle hint? What's a girl to do, I ask you, what's a girl to do?

Sigh. It's an age-old question. Who should pursue whom? I grew up with pictures in my head of a bold, courageous pseudo knight-in-shining-armor fighting some huge pseudo-dragon to rescue me. Then I was met with reality.

I would meet guys I liked, and I would hope and pray that they would try out for the knight-in-shining-armor role from my over-active imagination. The problem was, the guys I liked didn't always know that I was picturing them as pseudo-knights. I guess for a while I expected them to read my mind and zone in on my thoughts of attraction for them with some super-powered laser beam discernment from God. Sounds a bit like a cheesy Star Wars plot, doesn't it? Sometimes my imagination resembles movie plots, I suppose.

Looking at how I act sometimes though, I can see where it would be hard for guys to know whether or not I like them. Let me give you an example: I joke around with all of my guy-friends, especially the ones I'm comfortable with. The guys I like? Well, I joke around with them too, only I call it flirting. I also get really shy around some of the guys I like, so I *don't* joke around with them as much.

The poor guys. How are they supposed to figure that out? It must be hard for some of them to distinguish between joking around as buddies and romantic interest. And I *know* I'm not the only girl who sends a few mixed or confusing signals.

It's no wonder that some guys are a little "gun-shy" when it comes to asking girls on a date. Guys are taking a huge risk when they ask a girl out, and no one likes to get rejected. So what should we girls do? Do we pursue the guy? Do we ask him out? Do we wait for him to make the first move?

Some girls have personal beliefs about waiting for the right guy to pursue them. Other girls don't mind taking the initiative and calling a guy first. I have talked to many of my friends who have great marriages, and their stories are all different.

My friend Cristy tells about her first encounter with the man who would become her husband, Cullen. After meeting at a friend's party, they ended up sitting on a porch swing and talking. At the end of the evening, Cristy leaned over and said, "Well, I guess I'll let you take me to dinner!" That was just her personality, and she knew there was no way Cullen would ever work up the nerve to ask her out otherwise. Years later, they have a great relationship and she still laughs about how they first met.

That was great for Cristy, but I've never been one to ask a guy out, so what should I do? How am I supposed to let a guy know that I like him without looking silly? It's *so* frustrating when I like a guy and he doesn't realize it. The funny thing is, as I sat pondering this topic at a local coffee shop, I got an unexpected opinion on the matter from a complete stranger.

There I sat, typing away on my computer and trying to figure out the meaning of it all, when I overheard a guy and a girl at the next table having an animated discussion—no, not the Disney kind. Well, I'm not much of an eavesdropper, but sometimes I just can't help myself. I heard one of them mention flirting, dating, when to pursue, and how to know if a guy likes you, and I was all ears. I finally decided to risk rudeness, and I pulled up a chair to their table and introduced myself.

53

It turns out that my new-found friends, Andrea and Daniel, were college students on break. And Daniel was open to discussing the topic of dating. *Aha, I thought, a chance to get inside the mind of a guy for a few minutes.* I joined in with Andrea in voicing my questions and frustration and insisted that Daniel give us the low-down on boys and flirting. Daniel gathered his thoughts for a second and then spoke on behalf of males everywhere:

> Girls are confusing, and guys are oblivious. It's hard to tell if a girl likes us if she's flirting with us and flirting with other guys in the same way. We're more than willing to pursue a girl if we think there's a chance, but sometimes we need an obvious clue or signal that the girl is interested. We don't get hints very well. So if a girl is interested, there has to be a *unique* flirtation. She needs to give us some special attention that she doesn't give other guys. Then when we see obvious interest, we will ask the girl out if we like her.

"Well, what happens if I show interest and the guy doesn't like me?" I asked. Daniel looked at me like I should know that answer already. "Simple," he said, "he won't ask you out. And if you show interest for a long time and he doesn't ask you out, it's probably time to move on to the next guy." Ouch. I was afraid of that. But it did give me some affirmation about what I already suspected—that guys are trying to read signals from us girls just like we're trying to read signals from them.

To wrap it up, whether or not you choose to pursue a guy, at least let him know that you're interested in him. Come on, there's nothing wrong with a little flirting. Give the guy some special attention. Good grief, at least smile at him when he's around.

54

I'm not saying track the guy like a bassett hound and latch onto him like a leech. Just try to give some signal that you're interested. It takes a lot of nerve to ask a girl out, and some guys need more than a bit of a hint. You never know when your guy is waiting for some sign that you like him so that he can get up the courage to ask you out.

Things I've Learned: Give a guy some signal that you like him.

"I like you" signals

- Take some time to go over and talk to him—get on his radar

- Try saying: "I like hanging out with you," or "You're fun to hang out with."

- Compliment him: "You're so smart at....that's really cool" or "You're really good at..."

- Laugh at his jokes

"Let's just be friends" signals

- "You really feel like a brother to me"

- "I'm so comfortable with you, it seems like I'm hanging out with one of the girls"

- "I'm glad you're my FRIEND"

I always go for the bad boys...

I've got a confession to make. I like the cocky air that some guys have. The bit of a bad boy. I guess if I had to pick between the guy cowering in the corner or the guy kicking butt and taking names, I'd probably pick the butt-kicking guy. Now that I think about it, that's probably not the best thing. But who wants the guy in the corner? And you know what? I'll bet that's been part of my problem when dealing with certain guys. Take Sam* for instance.

Looking back now, I'm not sure what it was exactly about him that made me think I should follow him around like a puppy dog and secretly daydream about him. Was it his attitude toward life? No, not really. Was it the way he treated other people? Nope, that wasn't it. Was it his well-paying job? Nooo, definitely not. Maybe it was the lovely black eye he got in a drunken fist-fight or the way he was so gracefully fired from his job....What was I thinking?

> Why we like the bad boys: I think it's that cocky attitude that says "yeah baby, I can handle that situation, no problem. Your momma may not like me, but girl, you'd definitely have some excitement with me." We're attracted to that, but we want to change it. How crazy is that?

I wasn't. That was the problem. But guys who are completely wrong for me can still be very (and I do mean *very*) attractive. First of all, some people are surprised that Christian girls are attracted to guys *at all*. I have known some people who were shocked because they thought Christians didn't have any sort of sex drive—boy were they ever wrong! Unless you're an exception to the rule, asking Christ into your life is not going to take away your hormones or make the guys less cute.

So let's just be real here. The tall, dark, handsome, and charming bad boy walks up to you and wants to date you. And you say _____? Picture it in your mind, and be sure to make him extra-cute. Then give me your honest answer. I know what I said last time this happened, and it wasn't "Are you a holy man of God, because if not, I'm not in the mood to go out to dinner with you." I'll admit that resisting temptation is *tough*—that's why it's called *temptation*.....because it's *tempting*.

It's NOT temptation when the guy is scraggly and homely and you are not attracted to him. It *is* temptation when a *fine* brotha walks up to you looking like he just stepped out of GQ Magazine and wants to take you to a candlelit dinner. *That* is temptation. *That* is hard to pass up. Thoughts start going through your mind like, *He's really a good guy. I can change him. He just needs to be shown the right way.* Sound familiar? For some reason we girls always think that we can somehow rescue the guy and convince him to walk the straight and narrow. We think that if he will just date us for a little while, then he will see the light and lose all of those bad habits. But it doesn't happen that way.

Be careful about dating the bad boy to try to change him, it's a dangerous situation to be in. As a girl, it's very easy to get emotionally attached to a guy and even easier to get attached to the emotion of someone making you feel special. If you think it's hard turning down that first date, imagine how hard it will be to get out of the relationship a year down the road when you see that he's not going to magically change. I'm not saying you can't try to be a good influence on the guy, but you don't need to be making out with him to try to win him over to the straight and narrow path—although it *is* a nice thought—you just don't need to go there. If the guy is going to change, he can do so *without* you dating him. If he won't become the person you want him to be without you dating him, he won't change *after* you start dating him.

Don't be surprised when you find yourself drooling over a not-so-right guy for you. The key is to not put yourself in a position where you will have to resist temptation—because you might not resist. I'm just being real. Don't go on those dates with the bad boy thinking that you can break it off later. **Attraction is as addictive as crack cocaine**[1]— it really is!

58

According to studies, when you are attracted to someone, your brain produces high levels of a chemical called dopamine. Believe it or not, it gives you a reaction remarkably similar to being on crack cocaine or speed. This makes attraction (or the early stages of love) *very* addictive.

And you just thought you never smoked crack...

When I first heard that, I wasn't sure what to make of it. I mean, I don't remember anyone ever telling me that dating was like smoking crack. Then I realized that it explained a lot about why I act the way I do in relationships— thinking about a guy all the time, even if he isn't the greatest guy, and not wanting to break it off with a guy, even if I know that he's bad for me. I realized that I needed to be more careful about what relationships I get into because they might be difficult to get out of.

Most people will tell you that breakups feel like going through withdrawal. That's because you actually do. I don't mean to take the romance out of having a crush on someone, but our biological systems make it hard to go out with someone we are attracted to for a while and then casually break up with them.

So beware if you catch yourself saying things like:

- I can change him
- I'll break it off if things aren't working out
- There's no harm in going out to dinner with the guy…a few times
- Once he sees how wonderful I am, he'll want to act differently
- He's not that bad of a guy—besides look what sort of guy

"Karen" is dating

- He just hasn't had anyone explain to him why he should change

You can pretty safely assume that how a guy is now is how he's going to be ten years from now. No, he's not going to change for you. You're not going to rub a magic prayer lamp three times and have your guy magically changed. It just **59** won't happen. He might change a leeeeeetle bit, but don't count on it.

Look at what the guy is like *now*. Make your decision to date him based on that. If the guy does change, it will be a pleasant surprise and you can re-evaluate whether or not you want to date him at that later point in time. If he doesn't change, you've just saved yourself a *lot* of heartache, anguish, and anger.

Things I've Learned: He may be hot, but he's not going to change for you.

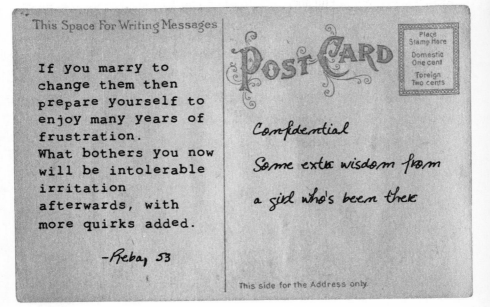

If you marry to change them then prepare yourself to enjoy many years of frustration. What bothers you now will be intolerable irritation afterwards, with more quirks added.

—Reba, 53

Confidential

Some extra wisdom from

a girl who's been there

If I could Just be Honest here.....

I wish that God would
Make you right
Whether or not
You wanted to
I wish that God would
Change your mind
So you could see the purpose
In it all
It's such a shame to think of
What you could do and be
It's such a shame to see you
With anyone but me
I wish that God would
Make you right
Whether or not
You wanted to

I think I saw a sparkler...let's make out

What happens when you're super-attracted to a guy and he's a "good Christian guy"? I know you don't want to hear this, but the fact that you're attracted to a guy is not necessarily a sign from heaven that you're meant to be with him forever.

I must admit, I once subscribed to this belief. I thought I would recognize my soul mate because of our super-strong magical chemistry. Sparks would fly and fireworks would shoot across the sky. I would be more attracted to him than anyone else, and I would think about him constantly. That was my theory. It turns out that being attracted to guys is a normal biological reaction, and I was attracted to a lot of guys that I *know* were not meant for me.

Yes, you definitely *should* have chemistry with the person you're going to marry. Do *not* marry a guy just because he's a "good guy," even though you're not attracted to him. You want to find a guy who gives you butterflies in your stomach and makes you giggle when you didn't know you could.

But girls, I'm telling you now—just because you feel strong chemistry with a guy does not mean that he's the one. I can hear some of you right now protesting: "But Kinda, this guy is sooo cute and I'm sooo attracted to him. Surely this is a sign from God. Surely I wouldn't feel this way toward a guy unless it was God clearly speaking to me."

Girl, that's not God speaking, that's your raging hormones talking. When you become a Christian you don't biologically change and lose your attraction toward all members of the opposite sex except your future husband. There are times in your life (and certain times of the month) when you just want to make out with any guy in sight who looks halfway decent. (Did I really just say that??) That's the way our bodies function. That's normal.

That's why you can't trust just your emotions and attractions to determine which guy you should end up with. If it were up to our emotions, we'd be canceling the Sunday sermon and making out with half of the singles group. You've got to *look for something deeper* than superficial attraction. After the raging hormones calm down over time, something substantial has to be there for a relationship to last. Who wants to wake up to a cute guy every morning who has a nasty attitude? And you don't want someone who is attractive, but doesn't really "get" who you are.

62

You've got to find someone who will be a close friend that you will enjoy hanging out with. You've got to find the person you're spiritually drawn to—someone who is going in the same direction that you're going. Find the person who gives you butterflies, but that you would still like to have as a friend even if the butterflies weren't there.

So enjoy the crazy giddy feelings. Enjoy the slightly obsessive thinking about your crushes. Then look for the guy who will still be the partner you want when he's grumpy, smelly, and sweaty. Look for the guy who has the characteristics that you would like to live with for the next umpteen years. Find that superficial attraction—then make sure you have a deeper connection.

Things I've Learned: Attraction to a guy does not equal destiny—look for more than that.

Things to Look for in a Guy

- Treats his family/those close to him with respect.

- Doesn't have a "playa'" reputation.

- Makes you smile.

- Has a positive opinion of females.

- Doesn't "fly off the handle" and lose his temper.

- Is HONEST. Being truthful is a character trait. Being dishonest is a deal-breaker. Period.

- Keeps his word. Trust me, this quality gets more and more attractive further into the relationship.

Apparently I'm triangle-shaped

"I started to change who I was hoping maybe I could get him back. Everyday at school for the first week we were over (after we broke up) I dressed so cute and tried to get the guy to notice me. I did almost anything." -T.M., 15

When you see a guy you're interested in, it's so easy to want to change to fit what you think he wants. It's not always obvious, sometimes it's just the subtle things that you change—like fixing your hair the way he likes it or starting to dress more like he does. That's fine for the most part. After all, why shouldn't a girl wear a cute dress if she knows that her guy really likes it? There's nothing wrong with that. The problem is when we start changing *who we are* to try to become *someone else* we think is better. The problem is when we start slowly changing the dreams and goals God has given us because they don't quite fit with the guy we have a crush on.

I have caught myself trying to change my dreams and who I was so I would fit in more neatly with the person I was dating. *It was like trying to shove a square peg into a round hole.* It would start innocently enough, with me just pretending to like certain things or not being quite as expressive about my opinions for fear that he might be offended. As it went on, I would notice myself questioning what I wanted to do in life and altering my goals more and more so that they would fit in with his plans. I didn't even realize how much I had changed until we broke up. Then I was like, "Whoa, where did I go and who is this strange chick that replaced me?" It took me a while to get back to the real me.

Why do we want to change for relationships? Maybe we just like each guy so much that we want to figure out a way to make it work. Maybe we're just not completely sure that there's a guy out there who would fully appreciate and be looking for who we are. It's so easy to fall into the trap of trying to become like someone else to "qualify" for a guy or to deserve love.

Here's how it goes: You're happy with yourself at first, and you're pretty sure some guy is going to be psyched to be lucky enough to date you. Then a few guys pass you up for a date, and you start questioning whether or not you're really what the world is looking for. You start thinking, "Well, look at Cindy, she always seems to have plenty of dates, so guys must like that kind of girl. Maybe I need to change a few things about myself."

65

Before you start trying to "fix yourself" or become more "marketable," I want you to consider something: *What if who and what you are right now is perfect?* What if someone out there is looking for the qualities you have that you think just aren't good enough?

> What if who and what you are right now is PERFECT?

Suppose for a moment that who you are— your thoughts, your hobbies, your opinions, your dreams of who you want to be—all of those qualities are *exactly* what someone is looking and praying for? You know, those things about you that make you never quite fit in with others, what if those things will make you perfectly fill a special need that God has? What if those things are what make you so special and unique that it will cause someone to find and connect with you? *What would happen if you change?*

The guy you're really looking for will not only *not* be intimidated by your dreams and goals, but he will *encourage* them. The guy you really want won't just "put up with" your love of God, your hobbies, and your personality—he will love you *because of them.* So make sure the thing that you change about yourself in a relationship doesn't change who you are as a person. Wear that striped shirt that your guy loves because it brings out the blue in your eyes. Just make sure you don't change your dreams and personality along with the shirt.

Things I've Learned: You don't have to change your dreams to find a guy.

I Think I'll be Me

Why should I be ashamed that I love to travel
To see diversity in its truest form
Why should I hide the fact
That the sight of a motorcross race
Makes me want to jump on a bike
And join in on the craziness
Why should I talk more quietly at football games
Than I know I would if you weren't there
I would scream. I would yell at the coach
Why should I hide that?
Why do I minimize my successes
So I don't scare you off
Why do I pretend to be less than I am
I've spent too many years being conditioned to
think
That the only way to be WITH someone
Is to BE someone
BESIDES ME
I won't do it this time
But I'm so used to hiding a part of me back
I don't think I'll know what to do
IF SOMEBODY LIKES IT ALL

I'm a seven-pound bass (in a vegetarian restaurant)

"Hey!" Zach* was whispering loudly from the row in front of me. I glanced up at the teacher to see if she had noticed. She hadn't. "How's it going?"

I nodded that things were well, and gestured that I was getting tired. Zach seemed like a pretty interesting guy. We had met in this class and had talked quite a bit between lectures—and sometimes during lectures when they were especially boring. It had become a running joke to pass notes back and forth when the instructor had her back turned.

But today Zach looked a bit uptight. "Hey," he said again, "I've got something to ask you. It's about prom." Well, I was awake now. Maybe I would get to wear that prom dress I had secretly bought after all. I looked questioningly at Zach. He waited for the instructor to turn back around and then continued. "Yeah, uh prom. Umm, so I've been thinking... your friend is cute, and she seems pretty cool. Do you think she'd like to go with me?" I sighed and told him I'd pass the word along.

Why do guys want to date some girls and not others? What makes a guy flip head-over-heels for some annoying Britney-Spears-wannabe but pass up the chance to take me out to a movie? I wish I could figure it out. I wish there was a list of things that I could do to guarantee that members of the opposite sex would be fascinated by me. It would be a lot easier if I could compete in a contest or take an exam to qualify for a date with someone. At least then I would understand the rules of the game and know what to study for.

But it doesn't work that way. Every guy is different, and not all guys will want to date me. Not even if I want them to—and that's tough to handle. Sigh.

When I find a great guy, I want to pursue him. I want to convince him that he should date me, even if he doesn't want to. But guys are not prizes, they are not goals to reach. They have different personality types and different plans from God. And they won't all want to date me. Or you.

68

I have learned that when a guy doesn't want to date me, it's easy to start thinking, *there's something wrong with me.* I remember having a huge crush on a certain guy. We had a lot in common, had a good time when we hung out, and I thought he might like me. It turns out that the guy never called and he didn't try to ask me out on a date.

I was crushed. Completely crushed. Crushed like a pop can on a train track. I had gotten my hopes up and expected that the guy would be interested. My first reaction was "What's wrong with me? Why wasn't I good enough for you? What more do I have to be?" The rejection stung like crazy.

I wanted to ask him what was wrong with me. After all, I'm a curious and analytical person. I need to know why things happen the way they do. If I have a crush on a guy and he rejects me, I want some sort of an explanation. Of course, I never actually asked the guy why he didn't like me, but I sort of filled in the blanks with my own answers.

My mind told me there was something about me that needed to change. I needed to work harder to make more money. I needed to buy more expensive clothes. I needed to be more giggly and girly and less tomboyish. I needed to *be someone else besides me.* I needed some reason to explain why he didn't like me so I filled in the blanks.

The reality is that sometimes guys just don't ask you out, even when you seem to hit it off. There's nothing wrong with you, they just don't ask you out—I'm not sure why. After all, this isn't exactly something that they explained to me in Sunday School. No one sat me down and said, "Okay Kinda, there will be a lot of good guys who won't want to date you, and let me tell you why." But after thinking about it quite a bit and spending countless girls' nights discussing it, I do have a few theories.

One theory is that I think God keeps certain guys from seeing what an awesome catch we are. Why? Probably because if the guy was interested in us, we'd date him. We'd fall in love with him. We would end up somewhere that was not our destiny. Looking back, there were some decent guys I would have dated had they asked me out. Were they right for me? No. Would I have been wise enough to get out of the relationship? Maybe not. So I think sometimes God protects us from ourselves, luckily for us. In the meantime, it sure seems like we're getting the raw end of the deal when we get passed up for a date.

Another theory I have is that sometimes we are stinkin' awesome, we're just not in an environment that appreciates us. The guys around us just aren't the right ones who really connect with who we are or want the same things in life. It's like being a 7-pound bass in a vegetarian restaurant: a *great* catch, but just not appreciated where it's at.

69

Finally, sometimes guys are just oblivious. Or scared. Or just trying to figure out what to do as much as we are. Guys are silly like that sometimes.

So don't assume there's something wrong with you when a guy doesn't ask you out. You could be the coolest, trendiest chick on the block. You could have a great GPA, be an all-state athlete, and be a kind, caring person. Don't be discouraged if the guy you like doesn't pursue you. Do not for one moment question who you are or what God has called you to be.

70

I wish I could give some of you a chance to step outside of yourself and see what the rest of us see. You are talented and unique (in a good way), and when your eyes sparkle with excitement, you are so beautiful that it makes other people smile. We can look at you and see the awesome, intricate beauty that you haven't even discovered yet. Then one comment or snub from an immature guy makes you doubt yourself or your worth.

Don't let it happen. Guard your heart and strengthen your spirit. Keep being you. Be nutty. Be shy. Be quiet. Be bold. Be crazy. Be dynamite. Keep being yourself instead of *reacting* to what other people might think of you.

Some guys just won't want to date you or me. It's their loss, because we're great catches. So keep your head up and don't change. The cute guy you're crushing on may not recognize the prize that you are, but someone will soon, and he'll be a great catch too!

Things I've Learned: Not all guys will want to date you— but you're still a great catch!

I'll take vanilla, Pepsi, and two scoops of rejection

There I was, bored and cruising MySpace, when I ran across yet another "100 facts about me" survey. Okay, I'll admit it, I'm a bit addicted. There's just something fascinating about reading random facts about people I barely know. It's like I'm sneaking into their world for a minute and hanging out. This situation was no different. I had only met this girl a couple of times through a friend, and I had only spoken a few words to her. But hey, it was a survey, and like I said, I was bored. I read down through the usual "chocolate or vanilla, coke or pepsi, who would you date in your top 5" questions, and then something caught my eye. The question was about halfway down the list, and it simply said, "Ever been rejected?" Her answer glared at me: NO.

I couldn't believe it. She had never been rejected? Never had anyone turn her down? Never had anyone disapprove of her? Never? Wow. I couldn't imagine it. I envied her. I tried to picture what her life was like and wondered if I could step inside it for a minute.

The reality is that most of us will experience some sort of rejection in our lives. Even a guy not being interested in you can make you feel like someone looked you up and down and said, "Nope, not good enough for me." And when a guy you're interested in turns you down for a date or doesn't pursue you, it really hurts. Even if you've built up your self-esteem and are secure in who you are, it still hurts. Even if you realize that it's not personal and the other person is just not a match for you—you guessed it, it still hurts. It can be a blow to your pride, ego, and even self-esteem.

People have been writing for centuries about the pain of heartache and rejection, and you know what? It's really true. Recent studies at UCLA have shown that when people are turned down socially they feel actual pain. During an experiment at the UCLA laboratory, some participants were left out socially during a computer game. MRI brain scans taken showed that their brain responses were the same as if they had been physically hurt[2]. Ouch!

So the next time someone gives you a hard time about being down in the dumps after being socially snubbed by a guy, let them know they need to ease up. After all, they wouldn't make fun of you for having a broken leg, would they? So take a day or two to nurse your "wound" (I personally recommend chocolate), and then jump back into life. And it wouldn't hurt to have a little chat with God about your hurts, as the next section explains.

Things I've Learned: Getting snubbed hurts ... literally!

Turned down again
Current mood: crushed

Rejection slapped me in the face
With its icy hand
I felt the sting
The sinking feeling
In the pit of my stomach
It laughed at me
Through jeering eyes
It saw my pain
Rejection came to call
To point out my flaws
I retreat to my corner
Shoulders slumped
Tired of fighting
And I let my guard down
For a moment
And listen to the faintest whisper
Running through my mind....
Why am I not good enough for you?

God, smite my enemies!

When rejection smacks you upside the head—when you've been socially snubbed—you don't have to lie and tell God you're doing fine. You don't have to make up some story about how great your day has been when you feel lonely or rejected. It's okay to be yourself and share your not-so-wonderful feelings.

Yes, there are times when we should be positive about a situation. But God never wants us to put on a false face when we talk to Him. It doesn't help anything and it doesn't make us more holy.

Did you ever read through the book of Psalms? Now those guys told God how they really felt. One minute they were singing praises of awe and glory to God. A little bit later they were crying "woe is me" and asking God to smite their enemies!

> *As for the head of those that compass me about, let the mischief of their own lips cover them. Let burning coals fall upon them: let them be cast into the fire; into deep pits, that they rise not up again.*
>
> *Psalm 140: 9-10 KJV*

We have the same emotions the writers of Psalms had, we just deal with a few different issues than they did. Can you imagine if the book of Psalms would have been written by some of us? People around the world would be reading scriptures like:

> *Oh Lord, great God of the universe, Matt is one hot football player, and he doest not see me, but he seest the stuck-up, back-stabbing girl, Carey. Open the eyes of his heart to see what a conceited snob Carey is. If that doest not work, bring a plague upon Matt and Carey!*

Oh Lord, you see my friend Stacy, she flirted with my boyfriend when she knew he was taken. Thou doest see the situation Lord.... SMITE HER, Lord, SMITE HER!

It's a pretty crazy thought, isn't it? But that's the realness of Psalms translated into what we deal with today.

75

So when you're feeling not-so-good, start by honestly telling God about it. I assure you, He's a big enough God to handle it. And the cool thing is, He *wants* you to honestly communicate with Him. He wants a *relationship* with you—to hear all about your day, your thoughts, your feelings. He longs for you to become vulnerable enough with Him to share your deepest desires and needs. That's what a true relationship is: opening up and showing someone else who you *really* are.

Be specific when you're telling God how you feel and what you need. If you're feeling lonely or a bit out of place, then talk to God about what you need. I remember one time that I had been out of town for a while. I really didn't want to have lunch alone again, and I told God as much. A random friend that I had only met once showed up out-of-the-blue and bought me lunch. It seemed small, but I still remember how special it made me feel that God would take notice of me.

God knows that you go through some rough times, and He's looking for ways to give you little reminders of His love. Kind of like little post-it notes left around your life with the words "I love you...God" written on them. So don't be surprised if God surprises you with a special pick-me-up when you're feeling down. Just smile and know that God is saying He's still there when you'd like to talk. He's still there when you'd like to tell Him how you *really* feel.

Love ya chica!

-God, J.C., H.S.

Things I've Learned: It's okay to tell God how you REALLY feel (He knows the truth anyway).

A shout-out to my homeboys

My friend Josh recently heard that I was working on a little writing project about guys. He looked at me from across the table at Long John Silver's as we ate lunch. "Now Kinda," he said, "this isn't going to be one of those let's-bash-guys books, is it?" I chuckled in between bites of corn on the cob.

"Now what would make you think that?" I asked. "I'm just trying to help a sista out here!" Josh smirked (I like the word smirk) at my attempt to sound cool, but still raised an eyebrow questioningly at me. I remembered that I had posted a few of my angry poems in an internet blog a while back, for all of the world, and my friends, to see. Oops. Now Josh was a bit skeptical about the slant of my book toward guys. I reassured him that I wasn't out to get the male gender, and that I would make sure to stick up for him and the rest of his chivalrous crew. I guess I finally sounded convincing enough, and he went back to chowing down on dinner. I thought of all of my guy friends who have helped me out over the years. There are good guys out there—even ones I haven't met. I just haven't found the one for me yet.

We get stuck in one environment sometimes (like the boxes I talked about earlier), and we can only see the people or things directly around us. I want to take a minute here to speak up for all of the good, decent guys who are out there. Guys who are praying and looking for the right girl in their lives. Guys who still believe in treating a woman with respect. Guys who are just waiting for the chance to sweep the right girl off her feet. They *are* out there.

Not all guys want to date Malibu Barbie, even though the guys on TV may make it seem that way. There are so many guys out there who aren't shallow and superficial. Just because you haven't seen one lately doesn't mean that they don't exist.

Let me give you an example. When writing this, I was curious about what guys actually thought about girls, dating, beauty, and attraction. I sent out a survey to a few guys to get their input. One question was: What is it about a girl that makes her attractive to you? I must admit, some of their answers surprised even me:

> "Ok straight to business.... What attracts me? Well I'll tell you: The first thing I notice is their countenance. That doesn't come from make-up or smiles, but God. Some girls who are shy have it. Others who are radiant have it. It's an inner beauty that people who are looking for it can see."

77

> "To me honestly what is attractive in a girl is her personality more than looks. I'd prefer a fun, easy going, loving & honest person as opposed to "supermodel looks" :o) Even in looks, if you want to delve in it, what's more important is her face & smile ;o)"

I got their point. There seemed to be a consensus that attraction was important, but that what they were looking for was more than just a certain shade of lipstick. Not exactly the superficial answers I thought I would get. (Sorry guys, I underestimated you.)

There *are* guys out there looking for girls who stick to their values. There *are* guys out there looking for girls with substance. More specifically, there's an incredible guy out there wondering where you are and hoping that he will meet you soon. There's a guy *praying* for you to stay strong and become the woman of God you were meant to be.

So keep looking for the guy of your dreams. Keep sticking to your standards of who you want to be with. Those good guys are still out there. And better yet, *your guy* is still out there.

Things I've Learned: There are still good guys out there...and the right guy is out there.

My Guy is Coming (read in a slightly
sarcastic, but hopeful tone...)
Current mood: creative

He's on his way, they said
From where, I thought,
Maybe I could
Start that direction
And meet him halfway
Maybe he was driving here
And broke down on the interstate
I haven't seen or heard from him
Maybe I should find a phone
And ring up Triple A
Maybe he's a little slow
God knows I think he's late
But whatever the case
I'll keep up hope
He's bound to come someday
And I'll hold on still to a friendly word
He's on his way, they said

Dating is a
BOGA

I'm more of a pit-bull
than a chihuahua

But Legolas never
argued with me!

Dating

I'm a duck...Daisy that is

I need a kick in the pants

I'll take a musician, please

THE TOP 5

THINGS ABOUT PRINCE CHARMING THEY DON'T TELL YOU IN SUNDAY SCHOOL

1. Prince Charming farts...a lot.

2. Prince Charming doesn't want to be Prince Charming, he just wants to play his Wii.

3. Sometimes Prince Charming looks (and smells) like "Old Toad Guy".

4. Prince Charming thinks a romantic dinner is buying you a hot dog...especially if he asks for mustard.

5. Prince Charming does not now, nor will he ever, notice when you change your hairstyle.

I'm a duck – Daisy that is...

Who am I anyway God? Am I the girl defined by the relationship? Am I the girl defined by the job, the car, the music, the clothes? I wonder what would happen if it all went away. And then what would be left and who would I be? If all the labels were gone and everything was stripped away, what would be left at the core? Because I think You're in the process of taking it all away. And I think maybe when I get down to nothing, maybe we can start again and You can give me what I need for who I need to be.

Phwack! The youth director gave an extra-hard tap to the sign he had just taped on my back, insuring that it would not fall off. "No peeking!" he exclaimed, seeing me try to look over my left shoulder. He quickly explained the rules of the game. Everyone in the room had the name of a character from a famous couple taped on his or her back. Someone else in the room was their match, with the name of the other half of the famous couple taped on their back. For instance, if you had Minnie Mouse, you had to find the person who was Mickey. But there was a catch. You couldn't look at the tag on your back. You could only ask people around you yes-or-no questions about your character. The youth director yelled "Go!" and the race was on.

After quite a few questions and more than a few frustrated guesses, I finally found out that I was a female cartoon character: Daisy Duck. Then I was on to the next mission—finding Donald. I quickly started looking around the room, "ducking" behind people to read their labels. My match was here somewhere. Now where was Donald anyway?

That icebreaker at the youth group welcome-back party helped us all to get to know each other a little better. Only later did it hit me that there were similarities between the "find-your-famous-person-match" game and finding a match in real life. During the game, you could see the tags on everyone else, but you didn't know who your true match was until you found out who *you* were. After all, the "Clark Kent" (A.K.A. Superman) I saw during the game would have been a great guy, and I think he's pretty cute, but how would he and Daisy Duck have looked together? Pretty silly. However, as soon as I found out that I was a cartoon duck, that narrowed my search down quite a bit.

I knew more about what I was looking for.

Oh Clark Kent baby!!

The same thing applies to dating relationships. The more you know about yourself, the easier it will be to know who might be a compatible match and who will drive you absolutely crazy.

Later, we'll talk about knowing your must-have's in a relationship. Knowing who you are can help you establish a few of those must-have's. So spend time getting to know yourself, finding out what makes you tick, what you really love. What is at the core of your being? Who are you when no one is looking? What crazy dreams fill your mind at night when you drift off to sleep?

Find the passions that make your heart beat faster and the hobbies that fill you with excitement. Then you can truly decide who your match made in heaven is. Then you can find the man who will help and encourage you to build these dreams and pursue your callings in God. Then it will be a lot easier to spot those guys you just need to walk past because they don't match where you're going.

Finding your goals and passions doesn't make you less attractive to a guy. It actually makes you *more* attractive to the opposite sex. Most guys aren't really that excited about a girl who's just looking for her "MRS" degree, if you know what I mean. They aren't that impressed by a woman who is waiting to take a guy's identity because she doesn't have one of her own.

Just this week I was talking to a guy at a car repair shop. (I'm a bit of a crazy driver, so my car breaks down every so often.) We had a while to wait, so we struck up a conversation. For some reason he decided to start telling me way too much (unasked for) information about all of the problems with his past relationship. I guess there's just something about me that begs, "Please, tell me all of the problems with the women in your life." His story went something like this:

85

> I think the problem was that the girl didn't really have an identity of her own. She would almost mold herself to whatever she thought the guy liked. I noticed when she dated me, she wore sports shirts of the team I liked—OSU. Then as soon as we broke up, she started dating the next guy almost immediately. What clothes did she wear? Shirts that had the sports team on it that *he* liked—OU. (For those of you who know Oklahoma teams, you don't switch back and forth between OSU and OU. You just don't.) She changed other things about herself too, as she moved from guy to guy. She never took the time to stop and figure out who she was, so she wasn't sure who to be in a relationship.

Okay, I *promise* I didn't make that up or put the guy up to it. He gave me that information voluntarily with no coaching. Guys really do respect a girl who knows who she is and who isn't afraid to be herself. So don't wait for a guy to build your whole world around. Start by finding out who you are: Daisy Duck or Lois Lane. Then you'll know whether you should be looking for Donald Duck or Clark Kent.

Things I've Learned: Find out who you are in God while you're looking for your guy.

Who I am:

_____

_____

Who I want to be:

_____

_____

Goals:

_____

_____

Hobbies I Enjoy:

_____

_____

I'm worth it
Current mood: determined

I deserve to be pursued
Admired. Sought after
I am a gift from God, a treasure. a pearl
I am someone worth fighting for
I deserve to have someone
Who sees me as the special woman I am
Who loves me more than life
But loves God more
I deserve to be treasured
A precious gem
I am worth the time to get to know me
I am worth your respect
I deserve to be wanted by someone of quality
By someone with dreams
I am a funny crazy girl
I am an intelligent steadfast woman
I deserve to have someone
Who's strong enough to lead me
I deserve to be loved, I deserve to have peace
I deserve to have the man of my dreams...
Find me

Dating is a BOGA...

Some things are black or white, but in relationships there are mostly gray areas. I always thought that things would be pretty simple in dating. I mean, what is there to figure out? You meet a guy, you go on a date, and God says "NO" in a loud booming voice. So you promptly break up with the guy.

Then one day, you meet that special someone, and instead of the loud booming voice, there are fireworks shooting across the sky and a big figurative neon sign flashing, "This is the chosen one!" Oooooooh. And of course, your heart pounds when the guy walks into the room and God forbid that there be any conflict or questions in your mind—because issues like dating are simple, right? *Wrong.*

Instead, you find out that there is a nice confusing gray area that just makes things difficult. I like to call this large gray area "relationships." In dating, all of those nice little clear-cut rules just get thrown right out the window. First of all, when you meet the guy from God, isn't he supposed to know that you're the one for him as well? Isn't he supposed to chase you when he meets you? Isn't he *not* supposed to have trouble deciding if he should date you?

Let's look at the things you need to think about when deciding if the guy is a match for you or not. In dating you're supposed to look for a guy that:

- Is similar enough to have things in common with you
- Has a common belief/value system
- Supports you and your dreams
- Has a personality that works well with yours

But what about the big ol' gray area (I'll call it BOGA) in each of those criteria? How similar in your beliefs should you be anyway? There are so many "brands" of Christians. People go to services that range from charismatic to more traditional. So it goes past "Is this person a Christian" to "Do they prefer the same worship style." That's where it gets confusing.

If the person you're dating robs a convenience store, hits his mother, or cleans out your bank account to run off to a small Tahitian island, that's a pretty clear-cut reason to break up with the guy. But what if you both just worship differently, what do you do then? What if he doesn't pick up his socks—what if he burps in public...a lot? Is that a big enough difference to cause serious problems down the road, or can you compromise?

I'll give you another one: What if he has a few things he's working on, and he says he will change? If everything in the relationship isn't perfect and you have questions about it, does that mean that the relationship isn't from God, or does it simply mean that you're living in reality and not in a fantasy world? Does doubt about the relationship mean it's wrong, or does it just mean that you're an uptight person?

The answer is......there isn't one. I know, it sounds like I'm chickening out on this one, but things just aren't that simple. Every relationship does not follow a set pattern. There is no formula to find the right guy. There is no "if...then" game that you can use every time like a recipe list, and there is no Christian Magic Eight Ball. There is no list of rules and superstitions to follow to lead you to the correct person, although I almost wish there were. It might make things a lot easier. Sometimes I think that there are more exceptions than rules. So don't feel like you're the only one who questions whether or not a guy is right for you. There *is* a gray area.

It's in the gray area that we throw away our set of assumptions and our cousin's step-by-step guide to romance and talk to God about the matter. It's in the gray area that we lie on our faces before God and cry out to Him in desperation. The gray areas reveal that we don't have all of the answers and we can't see the road ahead of us for the next ten years The gray areas force us to get our hands dirty and discover life, the good, the bad, the right choices, the mistakes. Most importantly, it's in the gray areas where we find ourselves and we find God. We find ourselves moving away from superstitions and rules and toward a *relationship* with God.

90

> *Trust in the LORD with all your heart and lean not on your own understanding; in all your ways acknowledge him, and he will make your paths straight.*
>
> *Proverbs 3:5-6 NIV*

So in the gray areas of life, take the time to stop and listen for God's voice giving you direction. Walk where you feel the peace of God leading you. God may show you a sign about where to go or who to be with. He has done so many times in the past for people who longed to know His will for their lives. Or God may ask you to follow Him through something you do not understand or to wait for His peace in what feels like total confusion. However long it takes you to find direction in the gray area, keep searching, keep praying, and keep desiring to *know* God and His way for your life.

Things I've Learned: God still speaks in the gray areas.

My puzzle
Current mood: confused

Helloo......
Any ideas, God?
About what to do
with my life?
You know I'm kind
of stuck
right now
in a tricky place.
Can't seem
to get out of.
So how bout
a little clue?
You know,
even just
a small one?
Like in those
crossword puzzles
when you're stumped.
And one word
makes it all
come together.
Come on God....
I'll even take a
letter.

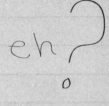

Dating Tips

- Relax and enjoy the process of getting to know the guy... he doesn't need to know every life detail on the first date. (So no telling him about your fourth-grade toenail fungus!)

- Compliment him when he does something you like. Sounds simple, but sometimes we only point out the bad.

- Don't make fun of him in front of his friends.

- Let him help you once in a while. Guys like that. And although you may be stubborn, you need it.

- Treat him like the person you want him to be.

- Be up front if something bothers you. No, he doesn't know why you're pouting. Either tell him or stop it.

I'll take a musician, please

I watched as the girl fidgeted in her chair, unsure of what to say. It was Monday afternoon and I had decided to watch yet another mind-numbing talk show while I ate a late lunch. I had tuned in just as they recapped the latest story. The girl had been single for a while, and her mom had been pressuring her for grandchildren. She had finally called the talk show for some "help" in the form of being set up on national TV. Now the host was asking her what she wanted in a guy. She looked uncertain, so he rephrased his question. "So," he asked, "what are your requirements for a boyfriend?"

This time she giggled and tossed her head to the side. "Well," she said with a smile, "he has to be cuuute. And maybe dark and handsome. But definitely good-looking." The host waited for her to continue, but she was finished. He picked up the microphone and looked into the camera. "In that case, ladies and gentlemen, I think we can find a guy for her today!"

I sighed in exasperation and shook my head. *That* was her only requirement for a guy? I could sense a disaster waiting to happen for this set-up. *Well, I thought, at least the ratings will be good for the follow-up story.* I took a bite of my chicken and let my mind aimlessly drift away, wondering if any of my relatives had ever called one of those talk shows about me.

There is a saying that asks, "If you don't know where you're going, how will you know when you get there?" If you think about it, that saying applies to dating as well. If you don't know what you want in a guy, how will you know when you do (or do not) find it?

Now I'm not talking about superficial qualities like freckles, hair color, or the sound the guy makes when he sneezes. I'm referring to basic values such as honesty, spirituality, and generosity. You need a standard by which to guide your search. Think about it and write it down. Many times I have said, "Well, I don't know exactly what I'm looking for in a guy, but when he shows up, I'm sure I'll recognize it."

Since then I have learned that there are some things that are non-negotiable. I may not know the color of the guy's hair that I'm going to marry, but I do know that he must be an empathetic person and he must love music since it is so important to me. Those are on my must-have's list. If the guy doesn't measure up, I'm prepared to walk away. (Or I *say* I'm prepared to walk away. Once in a while I need one of my girl-friends to help me follow through with what I know I should do.)

> Compromise on the little things - like where to eat on Tuesday. NEVER compromise your values.

I have also learned that when I write things down, it makes them clearer. It makes me think through what I want and figure out what's really important to me. As a single girl, it's easy to get distracted from goals or to rationalize why it's okay to lower my standards to date a certain guy I have a crush on.

It's called the "Yeahbut" syndrome. I start liking a guy and then I realize that he doesn't have the standards or character that I require. Then the little wheels start turning in my mind about how I could justify dating the guy. He doesn't have the same beliefs that I have. "Yeah, but he's a good guy." He loses his temper and has a negative attitude. "Yeah, but he said he would work on that." He doesn't get along with my friends or family. "Yeah, but did I really need that anyway?"

Writing down my must-have's helps—there's something about seeing standards in black and white on paper that makes them more real.

94

But what if you're already dating someone? Write down your must-have's anyway. Then compare it to what your boyfriend is like. It might give you some clarity about the person that you're dating. For example, you might find that your lists look like this:

95

My Must-Haves:
- Speaks to me with respect
- Values my opinion
- Is supportive of my dream of being a politician
- Makes time for me, even when he is busy
- Shares similar religious beliefs
- Gets along with my family

My boyfriend:
- Does share common interests with me
- Lost his temper and called me a *#$@!* idiot last week
- Didn't call me for a week when he had a paper due
- Believes in God…I think
- Keeps making cracks like "Ha, I don't think they let girls like you in politics…maybe if you sleep with someone"

See what I mean? It makes the situation a *lot* clearer by seeing it in print. You might keep telling yourself, "Well, he's not that bad of a guy." That may be true, but is he what you have been looking for—does he even have the basic characteristics that you said you require? Look over your must-have's and compare them to your potential or current boyfriend. It might help you know the answer to whether or not you should be in a relationship with that person.

Have standards. Write them down and keep yourself accountable. And as the next section talks about, have a friend around to make *sure* that you are accountable to your must-have's. Especially when you find yourself trying to change or ignore your must-have's to date a certain guy.

Things I've Learned: Know your must-have's in a relationship.

My Must-Have's (and a few Might-Have's)

Someone
To pursue, but not irritate me
To challenge, but not intimidate me
To have intelligence, but wisdom to use it
To show true compassion
To be sensitive, but be my rock when I break
down
To be the best of pals, but treat me like a
lady
To send me flowers,
But also take me to football games
To make me feel beautiful,
But also admire my tomboy side
To see the humor in life, to make me laugh,
But be as serious as the devil himself
When the situation calls
To be completely sold out for God,
To walk with the mind and heart of Christ.
To be my partner, my lover, my friend,
I won't settle for anything less
And I won't give up until I find that
Someone

Rethinking My List
Current mood: creative

I like my guys tall
It's true
Larger than life
Like my dreams
Strong and handsome
Saving the day
The heroes on
My movie screen
I guess I shouldn't
Go on looks
Or judge them
By their height
I guess I shouldn't
Look for capes
He's probably in disguise

I need a kick in the pants

You've read some of my must-have's, right? Oh, I've made them pretty specific, all right. Numbered them, put them on a flow-chart, color-coded them, and made a nice little one, two, three holy-hand-grenade list of what I need. Then the wrong guy comes along. I mean a completely wrong guy that I need about as much as I need Tabasco sauce on my breakfast cereal. But he's cute and charming Tabasco sauce (ooh, and a bit spicy too), so what do I do? Well, I have a crush on the completely wrong guy, of course. It doesn't make sense, and it goes against my logical better judgment, but you know what? I think about the guy anyway. You would think I would learn.

What really helps me here is having an honest friend who will give me a kick in the pants when I'm feeling swayed by the gorgeous hunk-of-a-man. This is *so* important. We all need someone in our lives to tell us the things we don't want to hear. We need someone to *keep us accountable* to our must-have's. When we're attracted to a guy, our objectivity in the situation flies right out the window (trust me). Our judgment can become cloudy very quickly. Here's a sample conversation from my life with my Annoyingly Honest Friend (AHF) not too long ago:

AHF : So, how has your week been?
Me: Pretty good, Seth and I went out to get pizza today.
AHF: Seth?!? Didn't we talk about him?
Me: Ummm….yeah…
AHF: Didn't you say he wasn't the kind of guy you wanted to end up with?
Me: Maybe
AHF: So what's up with that? What are you doing?
Me: It was just pizza….and a movie. We were just hanging out and..... talking....

AHF: Girl, you know that was a date. You don't need to get yourself into that mess.

Me: Yeah, but…

AHF: No buts. You don't need to get into that situation.

Me: Grrrrrr

As you can learn from my dilemma, it helps to have someone in your life to keep you real about your relationships. Make sure you let them into your life and share with them what's going on. And here's a bit of earth-shattering news for you: If you don't tell your accountability friend what's happening, then they can't keep you accountable!

The really good friends are the ones who are willing to tell you what you don't want to hear. They tell you what they know you will disagree with, even though they take the risk of you not liking them for a while. Why do they do this? Because they know it's for your own good, and they care for you that much.

The problem is that most of the time we won't listen to what's for our own good anyway. If our friends try to tell us about the flaws in our knight in shining armor, we put our hands over our ears and blissfully sing "la la la la la." If they point out red flags in the relationship, we jump in and defend the guy to the death. Our emotions and hormones are on overdrive, and we will ignore most good common sense to try to save a relationship.

Have you ever seen the TV show *Intervention*? In the show, there is a person exhibiting destructive, addictive behavior, and his or her life is spinning out of control. That person is usually in denial that there is a problem, even though it is hurting family members and friends. So an intervention is staged with the help of a professional. They confront the person and offer them help.

NOTE: Do NOT disappear from your friends when you start dating. You NEED them (and you NEED to have a life besides your man)

When you're dating, you're not in your right mind, so ask your friends for advice
— D., 21

100

Trying to get us away from a destructive relationship or guy that we're attracted to is often like trying to stage an intervention. Our friends may as well just duct tape us to a chair to stop us from dating the guy we're crushing on, because there's no way we're listening to what they have to say. We're not thinking clearly and we don't want to admit that the guy we like may not be the best thing for us. We just want to have the giddy, happy, happy, joy, joy, a-guy-likes-me-and-thinks-I'm-cute feeling a little bit longer. Us listen to reason? Now, why would we want to do that?

This is why it's so important to have people to keep you accountable while you're dating. As my good friend says, "When you're dating, you're not in your right mind, so ask your friends for advice." Trust me, these true friends are priceless—treat them well, and at least try to listen to what they have to say, no matter how much you don't want to hear it.

Things I've Learned: Find someone to keep you accountable to your must-have's.

Cows go moo. Ducks go quack.

I'm a hypocrite. I'm writing this section about dating, and in the back of my mind I'm hoping it isn't true. I almost don't want to put it on a page—I'm afraid it might become more real and I'll have to believe it. But I'll get back to my issues in a minute...

If a guy is *truly* interested in you, his actions will match his words. If he is really serious about getting to know you, his behavior will show it. It seems simple: If he says he likes you, something about what he does should indicate that. For instance, does he make the effort to call *at all*? Does he make time for you? Does he pay attention when you're around? If the guy likes you, he will try to get to know you.

There's a saying, "If it walks like a duck, talks like a duck, looks like a duck, then it must be a duck." In other words, if you saw an animal that quacked, swam, had webbed feet, and flew south for winter, it would be silly to try to call it a cow!

How does that apply to dating? If someone says they want to get to know you, yet they never really call, make time for you, or ask how you are, then how interested are they? Of course, there are instances when people go through

Quack? Quack quack?

difficult times or other situations that might make it hard for them to have a relationship. And it's true that you shouldn't jump to conclusions or assume the worst about a person. For the most part though, a guy's consistent behavior over time will show how he really feels about you.

The problem is, if we like a guy, we tend to grasp at straws to find any little indication that the guy might like us. We will follow a guy around for weeks just begging for him to smile in our direction—or maybe even just *look* in our direction. You know I'm telling the truth.

I'm right there with you. I've been known to let a guy just barely string me along while I rationalized why he didn't call or text. I have been known to make excuses for the guy I like and assume that there's some big reason why he doesn't act more interested in me. I would rather be naïve and insist that he has been busy rather than realize that he just doesn't want to make the time to call. After all, maybe he had a huge emergency and wasn't able to get in touch with me. Maybe he was stranded on an island and didn't have internet access or a cell phone.

Get the picture? Maybe I just need to read the signs and move on. In the end, I finally have to face the realization that if the guy *really* liked me, he would make time to call me. After all, I'm worth that.

My friend David has a great perspective on this. His theory: Don't spend your time or anything else on someone who isn't willing to spend theirs on you. If your boyfriend consistently acts disinterested and does not make time for you—if he disregards your thoughts and feelings—maybe it's time to look for someone who will treat you like the wonderful woman you are.

There are guys out there who will make an effort to be with you. Move on to finding one of those guys. Don't spend your time waiting around for the guy who says he's a duck but walks on four legs and moos. If you're looking for a duck, find something that quacks, swims, and has feathers. All right, enough of my analogies. Look for the guy who likes you enough to take the time to get to know you and makes an effort to show you how he feels.

Things I have learned: If a guy is truly interested in you, his actions will show it. Require more than a text message saying that he forgot your dinner date.

But Legolas never argued with me!

Script

Narrator: (Violin music plays softly in the background) You've found him - God's gift to women. He's perfect. He makes your heart beat faster and your world go slow motion, all at the same time. He's the perfect mix of George Clooney, Johnny Depp, and that really hot guy down the street you used to crush on. And he likes you. He really likes you! Sigh. Yes indeed, life is grand.

(SCREEEEECH. Stop the romantic screenplay! He just walked into the room and said WHAT to you? How dare he make such an insensitive comment and disagree with you like that. You raise one eyebrow and spin on your left heel to face him.)

> You: I don't think so! (said with attitude) Not up in he-ah!

> (Exit girl. Sound of door slamming)

And so goes the first argument with your "perfect" guy.

Ah, the reality of relationships. It doesn't matter how great you think the guy you're dating is or how alike you think you are, you will eventually find out that you are not dating the perfect man. You will also find out that conflict can be both a noun and a verb at the same time. I don't mean to burst your bubble about your perfect little relationship, but you *will* have disagreements. Count on it. Expect it. Be prepared for it. Don't panic. You will not always agree on everything.

It's easy to look at other people's relationships from the outside and think that everything is hunkie-dorie, as my dad says. Now I'm not sure what hunkie-dorie means exactly, but it usually follows "fine and dandy." I'm pretty sure I'm trying to say that things aren't always as they appear. Some couples look so cute and get along so well, so everything must be wonderful and blissful in their relationships, right? The guys probably bring the girls home roses every night and they never have arguments.

Just look at all of the famous guys on TV—they must be perfect, or at least close to it. I remember watching many couples over the years and thinking, *Wow, they really have it all together. It must be awesome to be in a marriage like that.* But I only saw brief clips of their lives in public or on television. I only saw the side of them that they chose to show to the world. I didn't see the problems and issues that they faced behind closed doors. I didn't see people throwing waffle irons and punching holes in sheetrock.

When I got older I started hearing about the weaknesses that some of the couples had worked through. I learned about their stubborn sides, their jealousy, and their bad habits. I learned that they had worked for years on their relationships to try to iron out their differences. Suddenly they didn't seem so perfect anymore. They still had good relationships, but they were not without any fault or weakness. They had to go through, and are still going through, a time of learning how to be flexible and *appreciate* each others' differences.

Any time you take two people who have different personalities, upbringings, thoughts, ideas, and goals, and put them together, there will be some misunder-standings. No one is perfect, so no relationship will be perfect.

I did find a guy once who seemed to be the exception to that rule. Six foot tall, blond hair. I ran into him at a movie store and struck up a conversation. The guy listened to every word I said, and his eyes never left my face. It was wonderful.

I tried to take him out for coffee, but the movie store employees kept stopping me at the door and muttering   something about crazy kids trying to steal the Legolas cutout. I guess that was the end of the road for me and Orlando Bloom. Sigh.

I have learned that if I want a *real* relationship, I have to date a real guy, flaws and all, and I have to be prepared for disagreements.

My "Perfect Guy"

The disagreements usually take some time to show up. When you first start dating someone, you always try to put your best foot forward, so to speak. This is fine—you want to make a good impression, and so does your significant other. But that means you don't *really* see what the other person is like until a while into the relationship.

Then you find that your boyfriend doesn't think or act quite like you expected. Differences start to appear and misunderstandings occur. You and your boyfriend are not as "polite" to each other at this point, and your true personalities and feelings start appearing.

When you start having those misunderstandings, take heart. This is the opportunity to see how well the relationship will really work. This is where you get to practice the dreaded "C" word: communication. One of the biggest ways to tell whether or not a marriage will be successful is not to see *if* the couple argues, but *how* the couple argues—how they communicate during conflict.

When some couples argue, they can take the smallest problem and blow it completely out of proportion. They end up making personal attacks on their partner by name-calling, bringing up past mistakes, and other "low blows." (Such as, "You'll always be a loser like your father.") By the end of their disagreements, it looks like World War III.

106

However, other couples find ways to deal with conflict that actually *strengthens* their relationship. They deal with the *issue* and treat each other in a respectful way.

So if you suddenly find yourself at odds with the heaven-sent guy you're dating, focus on handling the conflict in a loving and understanding way. Use it as a time to get to know each other better. You can learn a lot about a person by observing how they handle conflict and stressful situations. Look for the person who prayerfully and respectfully addresses issues instead of making personal attacks. See if the little problems turn into big ones. Everyone has issues. The key is to find out if your boyfriend's issues are the ones **that you want to deal with forever**. If your conflict reaches an unhealthy level or the guy is not respecting you, it's time to move on to a guy who will *help you face* struggles and not *be* your struggle.

Stuff to think about:

1.   How often do my boyfriend and I have disagreements?

2.   What are the things that my boyfriend and I disagree over?

3.   How well do we handle conflict in our relationship?

4.   Does the conflict ever get out-of-hand? (screaming, calling each other names, physically shoving, slapping, or punching each other)

Things I've Learned: There will be conflict. Find the guy who handles the conflict in a mature way. None of this yelling and screaming stuff.

How to Fight Fair

- No name-calling (well, unless it's a cute nickname ☺).

- Don't scream, even if he does. It doesn't help and it hurts your throat.

- Don't start arguments with "you never" or "you always."

- Say specifically what you have an issue with or what you would like changed. If you just say "You're an idiot," how can he change that? Besides, if you call him an idiot, why would he want to change?

- Watch your body language (arms crossed, mean look on your face) - it can cause people to get defensive.

- Use the "Sandwich Approach":

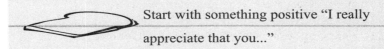 Start with something positive "I really appreciate that you..."

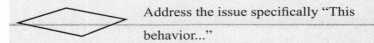 Address the issue specifically "This behavior..."

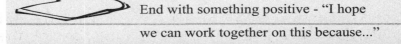 End with something positive - "I hope we can work together on this because..."

Good grief, is this a construction area?

It's amazing how much the little things will tell you about a relationship. And it's amazing what you can learn about a guy if you just pay attention. I remember my date with Blake*. We decided to stop by Wal-Mart toward the end of the evening to pick up a snack. I was hungry, as usual, and what was I hungry for? Chocolate—as usual. As we walked down the candy aisle, I spotted my favorite candy bar and pointed it out. "But I like this one," he said, and picked up the candy bar next to it. I'm still not sure if he had enough money to buy more than one candy bar. I only know that when we walked out of the store, we only had one kind of candy bar to share—his favorite.

Sounds silly to make a big deal out of a candy bar, right? But I have noticed that the little things in a relationship will tell a *lot* about a person. Sometimes people put on a nice game face for the big things—Valentine's Day, your birthday, meeting your parents—but you see who they really are when they're not focused on making a good impression. The seemingly insignificant things can speak volumes about a guy's personality and character.

Now I'm not saying you should flip out over a trivial issue—that just makes you high maintenance and a bit annoying. But go into a relationship with your eyes open and pay attention to what your guy does and says. If you see something small, make a mental note of it and think of it as a yellow caution flag. The small things can give you a sense of warning. People often tell you a lot about themselves without even knowing it.

By looking at a person's actions over time, you can usually tell what their values are and what they believe. Then by looking at those values, you can predict how the guy will behave in other areas of his life. You will often hear people say that you should look to see how your boyfriend treats his mother or how much he tips the waitress. That's because if he doesn't treat his mother well (a person he is close to and is comfortable with), he probably will end up treating you in a similar way. If he doesn't respect the waitress and isn't generous, those values will show up in how he treats other people in his life and in society. Getting the picture?

Let's go a little further with this idea. Some seemingly small things that guys do are actually warning signs of potentially dangerous future behavior. They're less like yellow caution flags and more like giant signs flashing "Dangerous Road Ahead!"

For instance, if your boyfriend starts getting jealous when you hang out with your friends and doesn't want you to have any guy friends, watch out! If he starts wanting you to change how you look, controlling how you dress, and becoming very possessive, beware. It may seem cute at first—your guy is jealous because he likes you so much, and that's adorable, right? What it can lead to is anything but cute and adorable. Guys who become abusive in relationships sometimes start out by being very possessive and isolating their girlfriends from other friends or family. If you see these signs, take a serious step back from the relationship.

You can tell a lot by the little things. Always be very aware of what's going on in relationships and be on the lookout for those little yellow caution flags as well as the big flashing "Dangerous Road Ahead" signs. Don't ignore them—they give you valuable information about the guy you're dating. Many times I have pushed the caution flags to the back of my mind and tried to ignore them. I really liked the guy and I didn't want to accept what the caution flags might mean. It was easy to rationalize the little things

I remember having a toothache and saying, "My face hurts." My boyfriend said, "Well, your face hurts me too." That's when I started thinking maybe he wasn't the guy for me.

-Glory A., 28

away. In the end, it turned out that I really should have gone with my gut instinct when I noticed the little things that made me worry.

Watch out for those little (and big) caution flags, and always take a step back, or at least stand still, when you get that "something's a bit wrong" feeling. Never ignore your gut instinct that tells you that something is off. See if those caution flags indicate a dangerous area for you to be traveling through. And (I never in my life thought I'd say this phrase) drive safely!

Things to be aware of:

- How does he act when he's mad—even toward someone else? He will be mad at you eventually.
- How does he treat other girls? What comments does he make about other girls?

Things I have learned: The little things mean a lot— watch out for the yellow caution flags and run from the big red ones.

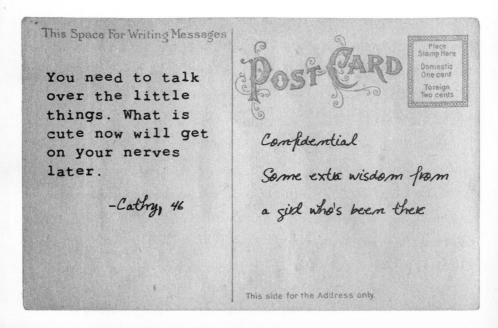

You need to talk over the little things. What is cute now will get on your nerves later.

—Cathy, 46

Confidential

Some extra wisdom from

a girl who's been there

I'm more of a pit-bull than a chihuahua

"Hey where did we go, days when the rains came..." I awakened in a bit of a stupor, trying to figure out where the music was coming from. About the time the song got to the chorus of *Brown-eyed Girl*, I realized it was my cell phone that had fallen under the bed. I never do think very clearly when I'm awakened suddenly; I always tried to turn off my glasses and answer my alarm clock. My friends think it's amusing. Anyway, I groggily picked up the phone and looked over to see what time it was. It was the middle of the night. Who in the world was calling me at this hour? Well, it didn't take long to find out. I barely got a "Hi" out, more like a "H—," and Matt's frustrated voice was going sixty syllables a second.

"What am I supposed to do? I like her but she's driving me crazy. If I don't spend every waking second with her, she gets upset. And that girl can get upset! She calls me every hour at work to check up on me, and if I don't talk with her for as long as she wants, she gets offended. She looks through my cell phone, my text messages, and the girl even hacked into my email account to make sure I wasn't talking to any other women. She's probably tracing this call too. And we're barely even dating. She's smothering me. I'm not a little kid, you know. I like her, but I'm not a little kid."

I tapped the cell phone against my forehead in mock frustration. I wondered what I should tell him. How could I explain some of the insecurities that we girls go through when dating? How could I tell him that we sometimes want attention so badly that we try to create it on our own? And what could Matt do about it? I wasn't sure. That might take a while. I glanced at the clock again. Well, at least I had free night-minutes on my cell phone. Let's just hope that I charged the battery.

Okay, I'll be the first to admit it. I have been known to try to control things in my life. I like the illusion of thinking that I can plan what will happen to me in the future. Any time that I feel I have absolutely no control (like flying on planes), I become fearful. I don't know what's going to happen, and it makes me uptight. That's why it is so hard for me to turn a relationship completely over to God or to completely *trust* Him. I end up making decisions based on *fear* of what might happen rather than *faith* in who I am through God. And if you think it's hard for me to trust God, imagine how hard it is for me to trust guys!

FAITH[1]   1. confidence or trust in a person or thing

FEAR[2]   1. a distressing emotion aroused by impending danger.

I have found that if there are any fears or insecurities at all in a person, they seem to come out in relationships, crazy stuff you didn't even know was there. You think you're happy and fine with yourself and life and then you add a boyfriend into the equation. It's like, "Whoah, where did all of these issues come from?" Things start showing up like jealousy, insecurity, worry, anxiety, and all of those other important psychological words that end in an "eee" sound.

Yes, it's amazing what fear will cause people to do in relationships. Girls will track down their boyfriends like a hound-dog getting ready to tree a coon. They will check his text messages, look through his emails, question every conversation he has had with another girl, and make him a call every 46 ½ minutes "just to check in." Yep, they've basically taken the guy's cell phone, turned it into a collar, and put the guy on a leash. It's like they're dating the Taco Bell Chihuahua.

Why? Fear. It's the tiny voice whispering *I've got to keep tabs on him; I've got to control the situation—If I don't, he might leave. I can't let him talk to those girls—he might like them better than me.* It's almost as if we think we're not enough on our own to keep the guy interested, so we need to follow him around and remind him, just in case.

But you know what I've found out? There is one thing that can't be controlled: other people. I can't make someone like me, and I can't keep someone from cheating on me or leaving. I have finally come to the conclusion that all I can do is be me in relationships. If that's what the guy is looking for, he will stay. If not, he will go. I can't control him, so I might as well calm down and just see what happens.

113

A guy once told me, "It's kind of useless to try to control a boyfriend's every move. If he's going to cheat, he's going to cheat. If he wants to stay with you, he'll stay with you. If you try to keep him on a tight leash, he'll eventually try to break free." Well, that was comforting and scary at the same time. That meant that if a guy didn't want to be with me, I couldn't stop him from straying. Controlling him wasn't going to make him more faithful. But it also meant that if I found a good guy who wanted to be with me, I didn't have to control his every move. I could *trust* him.

Now you know I'm not implying that you should be naïve and unaware of what's going on in a relationship. But if a guy isn't trustworthy enough to spend an afternoon by himself, should you really be dating him?

If he *is* trustworthy, loosen the grip on the leash a little bit. You are an incredible person—if your boyfriend is the right guy, he'll recognize what a prize you are. I know you just want to hold on to a good man, but that doesn't mean you need hold on so tightly that you cut off the circulation in his arm.

If he *isn't* trustworthy, then maybe you should be rethinking that relationship. Like I said, fear is a funny thing. It will also cause you to stay with a guy who *isn't* trustworthy long after you should have left. You have to move from a mindset of worry to a mindset of faith. You have to trust God and step out in areas where you cannot predict the future, even though you are uncomfortable.

That means that if you need to get out of a dating relationship, then you have faith that God has something better for you, even though you may not see it. And if you stay in a relationship, you have confidence that even if the other person lets you down, you are still strong enough to be fine. You have faith that while you *cannot control the unknowns*, you have a relationship with a God *who knows them*.

Things I've Learned: You can't control other people, and putting a guy on a tight leash doesn't work very long.

114

My not-so-good old friend
Current mood: nervous

I trust in you God
But fear slowly creeps back to my home
And knocks on the door
I look out the peephole
And debate whether or not I should answer
He's an old friend and
I'd like to see him again
I know it's time to move on
To a better choice of company
I know it's time to mature
And face this battle alone
But I still wish someone were here
To help me out
I take a deep breath to calm my nerves
And turn away from the door
I can still feel that he's there but I
Need to live my life without him
So minute by minute I keep going
And slowly but surely,
I choose God over fear

Don't buy the fake Fendi!

I watched The Notebook tonight...again. I cried like a baby. I couldn't handle it—watching what lengths one man would go to for the woman he loved. Does that even happen in real life anymore? In the movie the main character wrote a letter every day for 365 days to try to win the girl's heart. And here I am trying to convince a guy that he should call me more than once a week. Something's off here. Somehow my idea of love has gotten so watered down that I have become willing to accept a dime-store version of the real thing. I've settled for half-hearted attempts and fair-weather friendliness. But it's not worth it. If I can't have the real thing, it's not worth it anymore. And I'll wait until I find it.

Don't get discouraged if it takes a while to find the right guy for you. You have crazy wonderful things that you need to accomplish in life, and not just anyone will work. It might not take very long to find someone who's just "a good guy" or "a guy who has a job." However, when you try to find a guy who is not only attractive to you but also has a compatible personality and value system, it can get a bit frustrating.

After a while, the thought might cross your mind that maybe you should just settle and find an "Average Joe" to go out with. At times I have wished to be Average Jane—someone who fit in everywhere, blended in, and lived the "normal" life. I could be Average Jane, marry my Average Joe, live in a cute little house, and live happily ever after. After all, Average Joes seem to be a lot easier to find than someone who has beliefs and goals that are similar to mine.

But you know what? Through my trying to settle I have discovered a little secret. Even if you try to settle for an Average Joe, it won't work out. As cliché as it sounds, you're not Average Jane, so why do you think you would attract Average Joe? Of course you can't find a connection with some of the guys–they're not meant to go where you're going. Average Joe may even say the right things or buy you the right bouquet of flowers, but it's not the same.

117

I was talking to my friend, Cathy, the other day about a relationship of mine that had ended. She encouraged me to wait for the right guy. "After all," she said, "you don't want to end up with the *wrong* guy forever, do you?"

I thought for a second. "Just *how wrong* is the guy?" I asked. It caught her off guard, because she wasn't expecting that answer. I was joking with her, but my comment had an element of truth in it. It was tempting to want to settle for not-quite right, *as long as the not-quite right wasn't so bad.*

Not-quite-right may seem acceptable in the short-run, but think about what happens over the course of a lifetime. Think about spending the next thirty years with a person that isn't quite what you're looking for. All you need to do is speak with a person that is in, or has just gotten out of, a bad marriage relationship. They will tell you over and over again to take your time to find the right person.

You don't want the cheap imitation of what God has for you; you want the designer original. There is a difference. Designer shoes and cheap plastic ones may look the same from a distance, but one is created to last, built with quality workmanship….and you can afford it. You don't need the fake Fendi (that is spelled suspiciously like "Fondu" and is sold out of some guy named Herbert's backpack). You are worth an original.

God doesn't plan for you to have a "fixer-upper" mate—someone not-quite-right, but that you can "be okay with" if you fix him up. No matter how much the guy resembles what you're looking for, *it won't work out like it's supposed to.* There is something that will be missing; a spiritual connection that will not be there. Something will not feel right. You will not have peace about the situation. Do not ignore those feelings about something not being right. Do not dismiss your uneasiness as normal. Seriously consider and pray about what you're feeling.

In fact, I will go further than that. I will even say that if you do not have peace about a relationship, *you do not need to come up with a reason to end it.* I know every Susie, Sam, and Sheniqua will try to stick their nose in your business and quiz you about why you didn't stick with the guy. It doesn't matter. You don't need to have a reason to give them. If you have prayed about a relationship and you *consistently* feel like something is off, I give you permission to get out of it. It doesn't matter if he has treated you okay, and it doesn't matter if he's a "good guy." It doesn't matter if you've dated three months or three years. If you keep feeling that something is not right, walk away. You need to find God's best for your life, not just something that resembles it.

118

Imitation is fine if you want to save money on shoes or cheese, but go ahead and spend the extra prayer, searching, and discerning, and get God's original for the relationship in your life.

> *Delight yourself in the LORD and he will give you the desires of your heart.*
>
> *Psalms 37:4 NIV*

This may mean that you have to pass up several "bargains" along the way—you know, like the "bargain" shoes that don't match anything but you bought just because they were cheap—but in the end, it will be worth it. You will find the original.

Things I've Learned: Sometimes you want to settle, and sometimes you wish you could., but you don't have to

I want to settle
Give in to everything I've wanted
Live at lower levels than I can
I'm tired of working hard for this
Living up to this
Waiting for this
I'm weary from always trying
But never getting anywhere
I want to settle
Be less than myself
I wonder if the world would care
I wonder if I'd fit in there
And find the place that I'm supposed to be
I want to settle for less
Than the perfect guy
And have someone to keep me warm at night
I almost think that I
Would give up a little "special"
And be normal for a day
Just to have a loving hand beside me
Just to have a caring man that likes me
I want to settle

Right doesn't
mean happy

I've been slam-
dumped!

Sale and breakup
on aisle 5

Breakups –the Real Deal

Guys are like gangrene

THE TOP 5

SIGNS YOUR RELATIONSHIP MIGHT BE OVER

1. The new smash country hit, written by your guy, is suspiciously called "I'm Glad I'm Over (insert your name here)"

2. You run across all of the Valentine's Day and birthday presents that you bought him for sale on eBay.

3. He enjoys the concert tickets you bought him...with another girl.

4. Your friend runs across his new profile on match.com.

5. His facebook relationship status had been changed to "Soooo Over."

Sale and breakup on aisle 5

Sara* looked at me in weary frustration. Her earlier near-panic had calmed to what was now more of a frazzled, worn-out simmer. "I don't know what to do," she said in a tired voice. "He's a good guy, but something's not there. I don't think he's the guy for me. It's going to hurt him if I end it, but I don't want to lead him on. What should I do?" She sighed and leaned back against the couch, staring past the TV screen at some imaginary spot on the wall.

We had been discussing Sara's situation off and on for the past twenty hours at least. I started to add a comment and then caught myself. As I looked over at her, I realized that Sara didn't need my two-cents. I knew what she needed to do, and I knew that she knew it, too. And what's more, she knew that I knew she knew. Whew, well I guess everyone knew a lot, but we just wanted to ignore it for a while. Sara wouldn't see her boyfriend for another couple of days, and she wanted to talk to him in person about the situation. For now, she just needed to talk it out a little more, and I just needed to be a friend. I wondered about my ice-cream supply in the freezer. If she was getting ready to break up with her boyfriend, I might need to stock up on some more cherry-chocolate-fudge.

Ending a relationship—that's a tough one. Maybe you've dated for a while and you're starting to see that your relationship may not be as heaven-sent as you thought it was. In fact, you're starting to think it was sent from somewhere else. And your dream guy is looking more like a nightmare. You've decided it's finally time to move on. But how do you let him know that? Enter the different options: good old face-to-face meeting, write it in the school newspaper, announce it over the loudspeaker at Wal-Mart...I can hear it now: "Attention customers, would Jon please come to the front? Sara would like to break up with you. I repeat, blue-light special on the towels and Jon please come to the checkout to get dumped..." Wow, the possibilities are endless. And what about using new technology? That brings up another whole list of options.

Technology in itself is great. My new cell phone has become a permanent fixture in my life. I can sit in class and secretly text-message when I get bored. I've gotten so attached to my phone that I get a strange shortness of breath at the thought of being without that beautiful little piece of technology for more than a day. Technology makes it tempting to take the easy way out during a breakup.

124

As a girl, you don't want to hurt someone's feelings, especially if that someone is a really good guy you're close to. You just wish the situation would go away so you wouldn't have to deal with it. You don't want to cope with the uncomfortable emotions of seeing the hurt on the other person's face. You don't want to have to explain your reasoning and answer questions. You just want to take the easy way out and maybe even avoid the whole situation altogether.

Don't do it! If you really respect you current boyfriend, you won't let him find out that the relationship has ended by seeing you with another guy. Have enough courage to tell him to his face that you feel you should no longer be a couple. Will it still be uncomfortable? Yes. But it's better to end the relationship in a respectful way than to post a breakup comment on facebook or start dating someone else. Anyone who has been through that will tell you that it feels insulting. It's like you weren't even worth the effort to be told in a considerate way that things were over.

Side note: You can't break up with a guy and then flirt with him the next week. That sends MIXED SIGNALS and is confusing.

However, you don't want to keep draaaaagging it out just because you're chicken. The conversation won't get easier as time goes on. You'll just feel awkward every time he calls you "sweetums" or talks about how great you are. So if you know it should be over, do what's best and end it as painlessly as possible.

Now if you're in a situation with abuse, stalking, or some other "please get this crazy psycho-punk away from me" scenario, you might be able to skip the whole polite breakup scene. But if you're dating a good, decent guy, he probably deserves to find out that the relationship is over through you (and not your new "special friend").

125

As a side note, if you do happen to be one of those people who got dumped through an instant message or in another questionable way, don't take it personally that the guy didn't to talk to you directly. Chalk it up to him being afraid. Chalk it up to him not wanting to face a situation. And who needs a guy that handles a situation in that way anyway, right? Not you!

So if you decide your Prince Charming has turned back into a toad and you need to keep truckin' down the road (hey, that rhymes), try to give the guy enough respect to break up with him in a decent way. Be honest with him and let him know what's going on. Be *very* clear about not wanting to date, otherwise you might give the guy hope that he still has a chance with you. You don't want to be stringing him along for the next year if you're not interested—that's just not right. So keep it short, sweet, and straightforward. And remember: "Thou shall not IM a breakup letter!"

Things I've Learned: Be classy and keep breakup speeches short, sweet, and straightforward.

Breakup Tips

- Jot down some notes ahead of time about what you want to say. If you get flustered (as I do), you can refer to them and keep yourself on track. Or if you have a complete breakdown during the conversation, you can always just hand him the paper and cry.

- Be short and sweet and to the point. He doesn't need to hear how your aunt's cousin's puppy dog affected your decision-making.

- Keep it simple, like "We shouldn't see each other any more."

- Don't make promises of being friends forever. You probably won't be. At least not right away.

- Don't get into the blame game. It only confuses things. Just keep referring back to your original line "This isn't working out. We shouldn't see each other any more."

Right doesn't mean happy

It was obvious that the relationship should have ended. Actually, it probably should have been over months ago. But sometimes people drag things out a little longer than they should in hopes that it will work out. I sat talking with my friend about this particular relationship situation. "I miss her so much," he said as he looked at me miserably. "What am I going to do? I haven't talked to her in 45 hours!"

I smiled knowingly. "Luke*," I said, "I seem to remember you complaining for the last three months about how horrible the relationship was. You argued all of the time, and you had a *lot* of issues about some of the things that she did."

He sighed. "I know, but I miss her. I really liked her. Maybe it wasn't that bad. Maybe I should call her. Maybe I should beg her to talk to me some more. Aaahhh! What am I going to do?" I shook my head slowly and patted him on the shoulder. It was going to be a long week.

I have discovered a nasty little secret about breakups. I hate to break it to you girls, but no matter who ends the relationship or who does the breaking up, you will still have to work through some tough emotions. And I mean tough like beef jerky in the Sahara.

Many times you become friends with the guy you're dating and you really like him as a person. Add to that the emotional attachment of a relationship, and it's *really* hard to get out of a relationship unscathed. Even if you know that it is God's divine and perfect will for a relationship to end, it can still feel like it's ripping your heart out.

Which brings us to another myth: the "It's the right thing, so I should be happy and get over this" myth. Just because breaking up with a guy is the right thing to do does *not* mean that you will be happy about doing it. It doesn't matter which person ends the relationship, you will still go through things like:

- questioning and wondering if you did the right thing
- feeling lonely on Friday nights
- missing talking to him on a regular basis
- wanting to see and spend time with him again

These are not necessarily signals that you have made the wrong decision. It's just part of the process of getting over a guy.

The first time I went through a breakup and really missed the guy, I thought something was terribly wrong. No one told me that I would want to run after the guy screaming, "Take me back, take me back, baby puh-lease take me back!" But it's true. You go through feelings like that.

So many girls break up with a guy, miss him, panic, and then try to get back with him. Over and over, it's like some crazy yo-yo dating process. The problem is, after you break up you tend to only remember the good things about the relationship. And you miss the guy. You miss him holding your hand. You miss feeling like you belonged with someone. And you forget about his temper, his jealousy, and how he ignored you when his buddies were around. You just remember the good times, and you really want those good times back.

Give yourself some time after a breakup. It will take a while for you to think objectively again. Remember the attraction, dopamine, and addiction that we talked about earlier? Well the withdrawal symptoms hit hard after a breakup. You will literally crave talking to and seeing the guy, and you will want to make up any excuse to get in contact with him again. It will feel like you're going through some sort of detox. I'm not kidding. If you were in a serious relationship, it will take some time before you think clearly. That's why it's a good idea to have an objective friend around. And that's also why you can't base your decision whether the breakup was right on whether or not you miss the guy. You won't be happy and chipper after a breakup, no matter how much you know that the relationship should end.

129

Go with the peace that you feel, and base your decision on that. Your senses may be frantic and you may feel like the world is coming to an end. Go deeper past those emotions and see what your spirit says. It's amazing how your mind can be racing and confused while the spirit inside you is calm. That's because the Spirit of God knows what is ahead, even when you don't. Your mind is frantic because it does not understand what is going on or how things will ever improve. Your senses cannot comprehend what is going on, but your soul knows.

So even when you feel like the breakup is bringing the apocalypse, check what your spirit says. If there is a peace inside you, a "knowing" that you are on the right path, then take a deep breath and ride out the emotions. Oh, and take it from an expert on this, you might want your friend to take away your cell phone, just in case you want to call your ex again.

Things I've Learned: Breaking up is tough. Even if you know he's not the guy for you, you will still miss him.

Man, I'm craving one of his kisses right now — I love him. It hurts when I don't get the same vibe from him... My mind knows anything more than a friendship is devastating, but my heart still loves him.

—J.S., 16

I've been slam-dumped!

Sometimes things just don't work out. I know, I know, I'm hearing a big old "Yeah right" from all of you. But it's true. Remember how awesome girls don't get asked out sometimes? Well, awesome girls also get dumped occasionally. There are no formulas for exactly what makes a relationship work. You can try your hardest and pray as much as you can, but it still doesn't work out. As logical as that sounds, it still *feels* like *you* are the one rejected. Even if there were obvious reasons why you broke up and even if the breakup was friendly, you still get that crummy "I was rejected" feeling.

And then there are the not-so-friendly breakups—the ones where your boyfriend's evil alter ego suddenly appears and starts treating you like trash. The ones that make being in a car crash sound pleasant. I don't mean your normal, cordial breakup—some of you have been what I like to call "slam-dumped."

I felt that I needed a new term to describe some breakups. "Getting dumped" just wasn't quite enough. Slam-dumped is something worse than when your boyfriend just ends the relationship. It's when the guy ends the relationship and decides to go out in (horrible) style. It's like he sat down and thought, *Hmmm, if I were to break up with my girlfriend, how could I do it in the most outlandish, ridiculous, and hurtful way possible.*

I have heard many breakup

> He broke up with me and then asked out my best friend. That's really what happened.
>
> -A., 14

stories and some of you have had to deal with some pretty crazy stuff. I've heard of everything from finding your date out on the town (with *another* date), to getting a wedding invitation for the marriage of your "date" and your best friend. Yep, some of you have been through some pretty cruel breakups.

Regardless of *how* a guy breaks up with you, it still hurts. To be honest with you, at first it can feel like someone just picked you up and tossed you in a garbage can. You might logically point out all of the reasons why you were not compatible as a couple, but it still hurts. And when the day slows down and everyone is gone, logic steps back into the shadows and your heart cries. It's hard not to wonder, "What's wrong with *me*? I did my best and it didn't work out. What's wrong with me? Wasn't I worth working on it some more? Wasn't I worth the differences? Wasn't I special? What's wrong with *me*?" You feel *rejected*.

131

Re·jec·tion[1] (re·ject)
1.   To refuse to recognize or give affection to (a person).
2.   To discard as defective or useless; throw away.

To feel rejected literally means that you feel useless or worthless. What an awful feeling. There is nothing as horrible as feeling as if you have no value. There is nothing more destructive than a beautiful, talented girl thinking that she does not have a purpose in God.

Don't question who you are because a relationship didn't work out. Take my word for it, you can do everything exactly right, be as holy as Mother Theresa and as beautiful as America's Next Top Model, and some guys will still break up with you. It doesn't mean you did something wrong or that you need to change something about yourself. It just means that for some bizarre reason, things didn't work out.

So guard your heart and spirit and be aware that the feeling of rejection can stick around a long time if you let it. Recognize that you are *not* a rejected person. You have value, regardless of your relationship status. You are worth a fortune! And the guy who passed you up? Well, if he didn't recognize what he had, I'd chalk it up to bad judgment on his part. Silly guy. He'll regret *that* decision later. So you stay you and wait for the guy who *does* recognize how great you are.

132

I duck my head and sigh. I know there's nothing wrong with me. I know. but I still wonder every so often. As I venture out into new relationships I hear myself thinking "Please don't look too close and see what the others saw. I don't know what it is, but please don't find it. Please don't get too close and make me like you, because I'm not sure I can go through that again."

Things I've Learned: Getting dumped doesn't mean that you did something wrong. You could be Superwoman and Betty Crocker all rolled into one and still get dumped.

Ticked off...or something...
Current Mood: Angry

The words that I want to say to you
Come flooding to my mind
In harsh tones and angry voices
Rising volumes and frustrated noises
Phrases that circle my mind- But find no outlet
Sentences that line themselves up - Impatiently
And grow tired of waiting
The words that I want to say to you
Come rushing to my mind
In rough language and coarse adjectives
In shocking phrases I'm not allowed to
Put down on a page, let alone speak
The words scream at you
They curse you in a hundred different languages
And a thousand different songs
They yell at you for hours
Until my mind is tired- and finally slows down
Then they quietly take their seats- And listen
To one small, unspoken question
Hiding, ducking its head in the corner of my mind
Somewhere from the shadow I hear it whisper
What was it about me
That wasn't worth the effort -
What was it?
And all of the voices are silent
And none of the phrases
Have an answer for me

Don't slash his tires!!

Ca·thar·sis[2,3] - [kuh-thahr-sis] - noun
1. The purging of the emotions or relieving of emotional tensions, esp. through certain kinds of art, as tragedy or music.
2. A release of emotional tension, as after an overwhelming experience, that restores or refreshes the spirit.

"She did *what?*" I asked in disbelief. "Slashed his tires. She was pretty mad. Just went and took a blade to them, I guess." I realized my jaw was hanging open, and I quickly shut it. Julia* had done that? Dear, sweet, chipper, always-had-a-smile-on-her-face Julia? I wasn't sure how to react. Tim* had cheated on her a while back, and I didn't know what I would do in her situation. Now I stood talking to Tim's friend, and he wasn't nearly as sympathetic to Julia's antics. Oh, I agreed with him. What she had done was out-there, was crazy, was wrong. All right, it was even illegal. But I'll have to admit, somewhere deep inside of me I felt a little smirk, and I think I even heard a chuckle. Julia had done what the rest of us girls-been-wronged had only talked about. What we knew was wrong but still imagined. What we had schemed, brainstormed, and giggled about. Julia had gotten even.

After the shock of getting dumped wears off (or sometimes *during* the shock), the anger sets in. If you got slam-dumped, it's tempting to want to get the guy back for all of the pain he caused. You're frustrated, outraged, and every synonym of "ticked off" that you can think of. Let's just say that wishing the guy the best in life probably isn't on your agenda. What *does* come to mind is taking your set of Chevy car keys and running them down the side of his nice new sports car. That would show him! I know you want to. You really want to. I know what you're feeling—but it's *not* a good idea.

I've noticed that with relationships, the deeper the hurt that I feel, the angrier I get. It's easier to show anger toward the other person than to deal with my own hurt. So when a guy does me wrong, I start picturing all of the crazy ways that I could get back at him. And I'm pretty clever, so I could really do a number to mess up a guy's life if I decided to!

135

But I always try to think of what would happen down the road if I really let loose and acted like an idiot. Yes, it would feel good for a few minutes, but what would the results of that be? How would my friends and family view my actions? How would that help the girls in my youth group? And besides that, acting like an idiot would make me look like the bad guy and my ex would become the victim. Nooooo—I can't let that happen!

I also thought of another reason to keep my cool and act mature when a guy does me wrong: How would other guys view it if I went crazy and slashed my ex's tires? Think about it—would it make me more attractive to other potential dates if I screamed at my ex in public and then keyed his car? I don't think that they would want to sign up for that.

Stay away from the alcohol!!! Drunk-calling and texting isn't cute or pretty. And neither is getting plastered and showing up at his house to scream at him. Nooooo - not attractive at all

When I get angry now, I try to find a way to express myself that will let me vent my emotions but not get me written up in the local newspaper. Your way of dealing with anger may be a little different than mine, but the important thing is to find a way to blow off steam in a not-so-destructive way. It may be crying and yelling to your best friend about the situation. It may be running, playing sports, writing a letter to your ex and then burning it (the letter ☺), or finding a punching bag and knocking the livin' daylights out of it. Find what works for you. Just realize that when the anger subsides, you're going to have to deal with whatever mess you made, so try to keep it to a small cleanup.

136

Things I've Learned: watch out for the anger after a breakup-it can get nasty.

I'm angry
Angry that I liked you
Angry that I still do
Angry that you didn't
I'm angry
That I knew it wasn't right
But there wasn't any better
And I settled
I'm angry
That I have to watch
That I have to wait
That I have to cry - and others don't
I'm angry
My perfect guy
May not exist
And I'll just be left alone
With my dream -
And an ice cream cone
I'm angry

Maybe the past will change if I overanalyze it...

I sat in my bedroom and looked out the window. I could see the squirrels outside playfully jumping from tree to tree, but my mind wasn't focusing. I thought back to that last argument we had. What was that phrase I said again—that one question? That's right, I remember now. The seven words that started World War III. Why did I have to go there anyway? But I knew better, the fight was about a bigger issue, my words had just triggered it. The thoughts kept spinning around in my mind. It was getting to be too much, and it was wearing me out. I shook my head in frustration and picked up a blanket on the bed, curling up in it and burying my head under it like my dog, Dawn, used to do. Ah, that was better—no distractions, just darkness. It was kind of soothing and peaceful. I took a deep breath and tried to get my mind to slow down. *I did it okay*, I thought, *I really did it okay.*

Have you ever seen one of those movies (like *The Family Man* or *13 Going On 30*) where the main character is able to see how one small decision or action changed the course of his or her life forever? It's a crazy thing to think about: our lives being affected by every little decision. That could cause a lot of stress if you think about it. But I do think about it all the time. After a breakup, it's tempting for me to look back at every decision throughout the course of the relationship to see what might have happened if I had made another choice. If I don't watch it, I'll start to play the "what-if" game:

- What if I had prayed more about the relationship?
- What if I had been more understanding?
- What if I had opened up more?
- What if I had talked about issues more?
- What if I had *not* insisted we talk about "that" issue?
- What if I had dressed up and fixed my hair more?

What if, what if, what if? It's enough to drive a girl crazy, but I did the best I could at the time. I tried my hardest to act in the relationship the only way I knew how. But I still want to try and figure out what I might have done wrong or what I could have changed.

I might have obsessed over an argument that we had, how mad I got over something silly, how grumpy I was one day, or a million other things. Why do I do that? I guess I do it because I want to figure out what went wrong so I can figure out a way to make it all better.

139

But obsessing doesn't work for me, and it won't work for you. Living in the past will only torment your mind. Questioning all of the details over and over will not help anyone. It will not change what happened. Besides that, you cannot expect yourself to do everything perfectly in a relationship—after all, your significant ex didn't do everything completely right, did he?

If you brought up an issue and it started an argument, don't beat yourself up and say that you never should have talked about it. If it was something that was bothering you, then you were right to bring it up, plain and simple.

Take what wisdom you can from the relationship, and look toward the future. Is there anything you can use from what happened to make you a stronger, more self-secure woman in the future? Then use those learning experiences to look ahead and plan a future course of action. That's the only way to get to where you need to be.

So for all of you over-analyzers out there, try not to rehash everything in your mind until it wears you out. Remember that if you're following God, He will truly direct your steps, even when you are not aware of it. If your relationship is meant to be, God has a million ways to put the relationship back together—even without all of your help! God has been known to play some pretty funny games to show people who they need to be with. That God, He's tricky sometimes! So let your mind take a break, and let God worry about the situation for a while. Work to heal the past, live in the present, and look toward the future.

Things I've Learned: After a breakup, it's easy to question yourself and wonder if you made the right decision. Go with the peace you feel.

140

My sacrifice - sort of
Current mood: conflicted

I give this up to You Lord
But my hands still grip the edges
Of the sacrifice I hold
I give this up to You Lord
But my mind still wanders back
To worry over things which should be gone
I give this up to You and yet it seems
My soul still gazes back
And my hopeful heart still clings
To all the things I gladly gave You once
And maybe if I listened more
And maybe if I trusted more
I'd laugh a little longer, Lord
And cry a little less

Guys are like gangrene

I can't believe I'm writing this in here. It started out as an offhand comment I made one night, "Guys are like gangrene." It was one of those late-night girl talks where you start sharing and venting and making up weird theories about the universe. At the time it seemed really clever. I'd like to blame it on a divine revelation from God, but I think it leans more toward just being my weird way of thinking and the super nacho supreme I had for dinner. But here we go.

The word gangrene is derived from the Latin word *gangraena*, which means *an eating sore*.[4] It is literally the death and decay of tissue or body parts due to insufficient blood supply. This can be caused by a bacterial infection (gas gangrene) or by non-bacterial impaired peripheral blood flow (dry gangrene). [5]

The gas gangrene can spread throughout the body, exposing healthy tissue to infection. The toxins literally destroy the tissue. According to medical sources, gangrenous "wounds should be treated ..and observed for signs of infection or failure to heal. Dead tissue should be removed to allow healing and prevent further infection."[6]

I know you're asking, "What in the world does nasty gangrene have to do with me dealing with a breakup?" Those of you who have dealt with particularly bad breakups are probably already ahead of me on this one.

There is a myth in relationships about being friends immediately after a breakup. Either you or your boyfriend will say, with the best of good intentions, "I don't think we should date anymore, but we can still be friends."

Noooo. You can't. Don't even try it. Repeat this one after me. "I cannot be friends with my ex-boyfriend *for a while* after we date." I have never seen a *serious* dating relationship in which this did not apply. I know you want to argue with me on this one. I argued at first as well.

After one of my breakups, I still wanted to talk to my ex-boyfriend and tell him about all of the crazy stuff that had been going on in my life. It was innocent enough. We had been friends for so long and shared so much while we dated that when something important happened, my first instinct was to tell him about it. It was my comfort zone. It felt natural. But it didn't work. Talking to him made me miss hanging out with him. When we did hang out with a group, it made me miss dating him. I found myself in an unhealthy cycle of emotions.

143

I would start to get over all of the hurt of the breakup, and then I would see him. It was like ripping a scab off of a wound that wasn't quite healed properly. I would spend the next day or two in a funk, feeling crummy and sorry for myself. And besides that, I still hung out with some of his friends. Every time I saw them, it would remind me of our dating relationship. You get the picture.

Then I had an epiphany (what you would call a "light-bulb" moment). To completely heal, I needed to temporarily separate myself from the parts of my life that triggered all of those destructive emotions. I needed to remove those things that brought death to my spirit and caused chaos in my life. It was like needing to remove gangrene-infected tissues to protect the surrounding healthy tissues and to allow the entire body to heal.

Still not convinced that you can't be friends? Think about it this way: after you first break up, at least one of the two people in the relationship will still have feelings for the other person. Chances are, one of the two people still wants to get back with the other person. Staying close friends often gives the person who still has feelings false hope about a relationship. Then one of you will eventually want to move on and start dating someone else. It will be uncomfortable for the person moving on and painful for the person who still has feelings. Eventually there will be awkwardness with the friendship and you will start distancing yourselves from each other.

I'm not saying that you can never be friends with your ex-boyfriend again. I'm just saying that if you were in a serious relationship, there needs to be some distance for a while.

So try the "just be friends" thing if you must. But if you still have feelings for the guy, it will be torture hanging out with him knowing that he is being romantic with someone else. It will be agonizing. *It will eat away at you.*

Then when you're tired of the cycle of emotions, take my advice. Picture the disgusting gangrene and separate yourself from the elements of the relationship that cause you constant emotional havoc. In desperate situations, this may mean you have to separate yourself from friends and hobbies for a time. It may mean you need to find another coffee shop to frequent. And it will be hard.

You will secretly want to go hang out with your mutual friend to get some tidbits about what your ex has been doing. You will want to stop by his favorite restaurant to see if you happen to run into him. That may be okay for a week or two, but if you want to heal, you have to remove those parts of your life for a while. Cut it off, let the wound heal, and then see if you want to jump back into a friendship later down the road.

144

Things I've Learned: You can't "just be friends" directly after a serious relationship. You've got to "cut it off."

NOTE: Driving past a guy's house once or twice = normal

Hiding in the bushes and taking pictures of him = A BIT MUCH....time to cut the relationship off, sistah

Ben and Jerry
are my friends

Sorry, I get motion
sickness

Moving On... Eventually

Masks get itchy

THE TOP 5

SIGNS YOU MIGHT BE GOING THROUGH A BAD BREAKUP

1. Your dog can recognize "Baby Please Come Back" from the opening chords and starts howling.

2. Baskin Robbins named its new chocolate ice cream "Bad Breakup Binge" in honor of you.

3. The movie rental store employees chipped in and bought you your own copy of Twilight...and a box of tissues.

4. Your hamster hides in its tunnel when it hears your ex's name.

5. Your sister wants to know where all of the headless pictures came from.

Ben & Jerry are my friends

Okay, let me give you a warning right now. The minute you go through a breakup, there will be a certain group of people, although well-meaning, who will try to force you to see the super-positive side of the situation. You know who I'm talking about: "I just heard what happened and praise Jaysus, the Lawd is bringin' all of this to you for your good. Let's just have a praise service right here and thank the Lawd for His divine work in your life—hallelujah!"

These people have good intentions, but chances are, you don't feel like shouting "Glory to God" when you've just had your heart trampled. Chances are, you instead feel like punching a wall—or punching something that bears a strange resemblance to your ex. That's okay. You're human and you have human emotions. Yes, God may be working it out for your good, but I don't think He expects you to be giddy about losing a relationship that you cared about.

You're mad, you're sad, you're sick, you're in shock, but you're probably not happy and jumping for joy. And you might not want to listen to inspirational music the day you break up, you might just hear Alanis or Avril calling your name instead. So I am going to tell you something now that I never heard growing up: I am officially giving you permission to get angry, sad, confused, and scared. Keep it in the back of your mind that God *does* have it under control. Then go let off some steam at the batting cages or by writing some angry music (a personal favorite of mine). Better yet, write down your feelings in poem form and then publish it in a book. Break out some angry girl music...grrrr. Talk to your girl-friends for hours about what you went through.

And then there's the time for moping. If it's really bad, stay in bed for a day and cry, cry, cry. For a while, I recommend just getting a big bowl of Kettle Corn, a large Cherry Coke, and vegging out in front of the TV. Helpful? No, but you need that. It's all part of the process. There is a season of grief in dealing with the end of a relationship. You're mourning the loss of a dream, of what you thought the relationship would be. You're mourning the loss of a feeling, a friend.

Unfortunately for me, when I get stressed out the first thing that goes is my appetite. So instead of enjoying a large banana split to nurse my wounds, I'm trying to choke down wheat crackers and cream cheese because my stomach is in knots. Shame on those boys—taking away my appetite like that. But you can bet that as soon as I can, I'm drowning my sorrows in a big ol' bag of Crunchy Cheetos and a package of chocolate chip cookies. Not the healthiest recommendation, I know, but sometimes it's just what the doctor ordered.

So do you stay in bed with the bag of Cheetos forever? No. Eventually you've gotta start moving toward some sort of way to deal with the breakup. For a while though, you just need to cry, write angry poetry, and eat chocolate. How long does it take? It's different for everyone and every relationship. Dealing with the loss of someone you dated for three years will be different than breaking up with a guy who just took you out to the movies a couple of times. So drink that chocolate slurpee for a bit and gather up all of your energy for facing the real world.

Things I've Learned: It's okay to let yourself feel bad for a bit and chug that cherry cola. Just know yourself and know your limits.

Someday

Someday this won't hurt so bad
But not today
Today I'm crying
Someday I won't feel this sad
But not today
Today I'm dying
Someday I'll be good to go
And someday I'll
Just show them all
Someday I'll find what I'm meant to be
Someday I'll find you and you'll find
me
Someday this won't hurt
But not today
Today I'm crying

How long does it take to get over a guy?
Some say half the amount of time that
you were in the relationship. But it sure
feels like forever.

Breakup Timeline (use what applies)

152

This isn't really happening - we might still get back together

I miss him soooo much - he wasn't that bad, and I want him back!

I can't stop eating! (or I don't feel like eating at all)

This doesn't seem quite real. I feel sorta numb.

What a jerk - I can't believe he did that!!

I need to see him NOWWW!!!

This is a bit overwhelming - I just want to cry. Or scream... Or sleep.

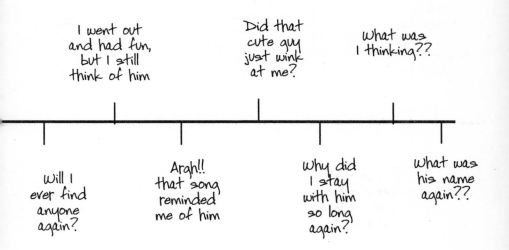

Pizza, Milkshakes, and Visa

154

All right, there will come a time in this whole breakup recovery process when you have to do the unthinkable—leave the house. Or even worse, you may have to smile and meet new people. Yep, you or your friends will eventually realize that you need to get out and join the real world.

This might not be easy at first. You will probably have to make a conscious effort to get out and socialize when you know it's best for you. When your friends ask you to go with them to a football game or to see a movie, say yes. You might not feel like being happy and sociable, but it helps to get out and make an effort. Just pace yourself. You might even need to find a new hobby or group to join (that doesn't involve the ex or his friends).

And if you're one of those girls who went MIA from all of her friends as soon as she started dating someone, well, swallow your pride and give them a call. Tell them you learned your lesson, and you won't ditch them again. Then tell them you'll even spring for a large, triple-cheese and sausage pizza and four large chocolate milkshakes if they'll come hang out for a while. You need them.

Things I've Learned: There comes a point when you have to make an effort to get back in the real world.

```
Things I do when I want to cry - by Tabitha, 16
❖Call one my friends up and say, "hey u want to
  hang out?" (We go make cookies or drive around.)
❖Take a shower and then figure a few diff ways to
  do my make-up and hair.
❖Go and work out.
❖Dance in front of the mirror.
❖Find something that I like doing and do it.
```

Masks get itchy

I had been at Amy's house for a couple of hours. It had been a stressful day, I wasn't sure what was going on in my life, and I was ticked off. It was all hitting me at once. I would start to discuss the problem for a few minutes and then apologize for talking about it. I felt guilty for not being happy and peppy, and I didn't want to ruin her evening. Amy had finally had enough. "Kinda, you only let part of it out. You start to tell me about what's bothering you, and then you keep the rest inside. I don't mind listening, and how am I going to be a true friend if you don't just let it go?"

I was so accustomed to helping other people out and listening to their problems that I felt guilty when I needed to talk to someone. I didn't want to be weak. I wanted to look like the good strong girl setting a good example. I didn't want to let another person into my life who could potentially hurt me.

I wanted to wear a mask. A mask that didn't let people see the real me. A mask that protected me. But I couldn't get the accountability and friendship that I needed by putting up a false front. *And I couldn't get help hiding behind a mask.*

That's what friendship and community is all about—joining together for a common cause, helping each other out in times of stress. Sometimes just listening or crying with each other helps tremendously. A person can survive without a network of friends, but if it is available, it is a gift from God. It is in our very nature to cry out when our soul feels hurt or alone. So consider yourself blessed if you have a friend, leader, or mentor in your life that you trust. Don't be afraid to open up with them and share what's on your heart. Don't be too proud to call them up when you're feeling down. Let them be a blessing in your life so you will be better able to bless others in the future.

So take a break and put down the mask. Everyone feels down in the dumps once in a while. And more often than we like to admit, we sometimes get "stuck"in the dumps and have a hard time snapping out of it. I almost hate to use the word "depression" here because it always seems to bring up a weird negative reaction in people. When someone mentions the word depression we all look around at each other with innocent looks on our faces and say "Nooo, not me." We seem to think depression is some unholy, nasty, God-forsaken plague. Well, I think it's about time that people got over that idea.

There's no shame in going through depression. Many of us have been there— about one in four girls in fact[1]! I just want to make sure that if you have to deal with depression, you go *through* it and don't get stuck there.

So if you've been feeling down for quite a while and can't seem to shake it, go ahead and seek advice for dealing with it. I think you'll find that a lot of people have gone through what you're going through. They can help you understand what you're dealing with and help you get through it. For example, when feelings of rejection or loneliness hit you pretty hard, you may face emotions like[2]:

- persistent sad, anxious or "empty" mood
- feelings of hopelessness, pessimism
- feelings of guilt, worthlessness, helplessness
- loss of interest or pleasure in hobbies and activities that were once enjoyed
- decreased energy, fatigue
- difficulty concentrating, remembering and making decisions
- insomnia, early-morning awakening, or oversleeping
- appetite and/or weight loss or overeating and weight gain
- restlessness, irritability
- persistent physical symptoms that do not respond to treatment, such as headaches, digestive disorders, and chronic pain
- thoughts of death or suicide

If you find that you have several of these emotions continually for a period of time (a couple of weeks or more), definitely talk to a mentor. They can work with you to help overcome it. Everyone needs a friend to help them out, and everyone needs someone to see behind their mask.

Things I've Learned: It's okay to let others see your weaknesses, so put down the mask for a while.

Tips to Beat the Blues

- Eat healthy foods - your body will be able to better handle stress.

- Find a good friend or mentor to talk to.

- Sleep enough. Our brains just don't work like they should without sleep.

- Try to get some form of exercise, even a brisk walk around the block. When we exercise, our body produces endorphins (ever heard of a "runner's high"? That happy feeling is from good ol' endorphins).[3]

- Put on some good "cheer me up" music to rock out to. Studies have shown that listening to or playing music you enjoy can have astounding effects, including helping to bring a more positive state of mind.[4]

- Find a hobby or sport that you enjoy and can participate in.

Things I Do When I Want to Cry
by "the girls" - ages 15-17

Talk to someone
Write in a diary/journal
Exercise
Listen to music
Cuddle with pet
Count to ten
Take a long bubble bath
Clean something
Dance
Take a moment for myself
Sleep
Stay away from other people
Call a friend
Write poetry
Play an instrument

Sorry, I get motion sickness

Ever ridden the Texas Giant? It's a huge wooden roller coaster at Six Flags Over Texas. I made the mistake of letting my friends talk me into riding it once. Of course, you can probably guess that I'm afraid of roller coasters and any other rides that throw me around through the air with nothing but a small metal bar holding me in a seat. But they dared me, so I had to try it. Let me tell you, it was like being in a car wreck a hundred feet in the air. It took me up, it took me down, it shook me all around. (Shake it, shake it, shake it...shake it like a salt...oooh sorry about that. I do get distracted.) I was holding on tight and making deals with God left and right. Whew, I did not look pretty when I stepped off of that ride. I looked like a Pomeranian puppy that had been stuck outside during a wind storm, and I think my face had a bit of a green tint. Needless to say, it was not fun for me.

The emotions you experience following a breakup resemble those crazy roller coasters. You might feel down for a few days, and then things will start to look up. Then you might hit a rough spot again and be down for a while. It will be up and down for a time. Don't consider it failure to have a few bad days down the road. This isn't a "relapse," and it doesn't mean that you're doing something wrong.

Slowly but surely, things will even out. Keep working through it with God. Keep walking it out. Out of nowhere, you will wake up one day and feel a bit happier, and some of the load will be gone. There will be less suffocation. You might have some more down times, but the roller coaster will start evening out more. The depressed feelings won't stay as long each time, and you'll start to feel more like your old self.

It will get better. You will get up one Saturday morning and want to go shop at your favorite store or eat at your favorite restaurant. You will be excited about where you are going in life and who you are becoming. You will find yourself laughing like crazy at something silly. You will even give up your notion that all men are jerks and want to start dating again (I promise). You will look at yourself and suddenly realize that you are okay, and that you will come out of this mess even stronger than before. You will realize that you are an incredible woman, and that you really like yourself. You will realize that you are enough.

160

Things I've Learned: Things will start looking up and leveling out; just ride out the mess.

Directions for a little pick-me-up reminder:

1. Cut out
2. Tape to mirror
3. Repeat every hour as necessary

There are other guys out there

There are BETTER guys out there

I will be fine

I AM fine (and foxy)

I am better off without him

I am better off without him

I am better off without him

I am enough

Final
Thoughts

Pass it On

I am enough

I think it has taken me a while to get this one down. I think I've got it, and then once in a while life will roll me up in sticky paper and throw me up against a wall just to see what happens. Then I wonder how well I've mastered the concept. But I'm getting there. Through everything I'm starting to learn the one thing that matters—the one thing that changes how I perceive the world—that I am enough.

Over the years, when guys would turn me down or not be interested in me, my first instinct was to chase them down and give them my one, two, three list of why they should like me. Now I just kind of sit back and think, *hmmm....well, they missed out on that one, didn't they?*

When people talk about their jobs, boyfriends, clothes, cars, or jewelry now, I'm happy for them. I feel less of an urge to chase after every dream or goal that everyone else has. I'm enjoying living *my* life. And I've come to the conclusion that I am happy with me. So if there's one thing I could pass on to you girls, it would be this: know that through everything, you are enough.

All of those things that you deal with in life—relationships, emotions, hormones, friends, enemies, parents—they sometimes toss you around, throw you off balance, and cause you to question who you are. But know that through it all, you are enough. Your dreams, your crazy personality, your talents and goals—they are God-given. They are enough. This is the center of it all. Everything, all of the emotions, relationships, friendships, good days and bad days, revolve around it. This is one of the easiest lessons to doubt, and it's the one I have to come back to the most often.

So just in case you missed it, let me remind you a few more times. You are enough. Just you. As you go through all of the ups and downs of life, it doesn't change the fact that you are enough. If you are crying to God that your heart is breaking, or if you are feeling unlovely and lonely, you are still enough. You will probably have many emotions that contradict this truth, but it doesn't matter. Just know that you'll make it, and you're right where you need to be.

You are enough. If you never accomplish what everyone thinks you should, if you never do what "they" think you should do, and if you never have one penny more than you do now, you are enough. Just you. You are enough to deserve unconditional love. You are enough to have someone think you are the most beautiful person in the world. Without changing a single thing, you are enough. You don't have to work at it, try for it, or stay up stressing about it.

Feeling down or ugly does not change your beauty, only how you perceive it for the time being. Emotions in life may take you away from seeing it, and relationships may contradict it, but that doesn't change the fact that all you have to be is you, and that is enough.

So put up with the emotions, be prepared for the bumpy roller coaster ride, and know that no matter how much life is tossing you around, you'll come out okay. You are beautiful, talented, and loved, and YOU ARE ENOUGH!

Things I've Learned: You are enough!

I Refuse

I refuse to settle for second best
I request, I insist, I demand
For at least the double of fifty percent
Of the blessings God wills in my hands
I refuse to stoop to the ranks of defeat
I shall not, I will not, I won't
Back down in the battle or cry for surrender
When victory lies in the front
I refuse to march to the drums of the world
That beat out gloom and despair
I will live by the rules of a higher command
I will do the impossible by prayer
I refuse to seek out the least in life
Or to half-heartedly saunter along
I refuse to not follow God's perfect will
For the wholeness of all that I am
But I will succeed
I will prosper in God
I will stand tall in cowering crowds
I will walk in the truth
I will live in the light
I will follow the not-taken road
For things I will gain bring fullness of joy
Perfection in God's destiny
And in the end I will look back and know
What I lost meant nothing to me

Pass it on

I had been coming to the Bible study for weeks since my latest breakup. From everyone's perspective around me, I had moved on, healed, gotten happy, and I was super-duper fine. My close friends had stopped calling me days before to ask how I was. No wait, I'm not sure if some of them ever asked how I was. But back to my story.

As I left the Bible study that Monday night, Erika* stopped me on the way to my car. I had known Erika for at least a year as an acquaintance, but we had never spent much time talking. She was in a different hangout group, and we had just never had the chance to really get to know each other. That night though, Erika paused as we stepped outside and asked, "So, how are you Kinda?" I replied that I was fine. She stopped me then, and looked me square in the eyes. "No *really* Kinda," she said again, "how are you *really* doing?"

It was such a simple gesture, but I will never forget it. A person who barely knew me put everything that was going on in her life on hold to be a friend to me.

Sometimes we get so caught up in our own self-created worlds that we forget about all of the other people who are hurting around us. We fail to connect with others and share in our healing. I have learned that when I step out of my comfort zone to lift someone else's spirits, mine seems to lift as well. It changes my perspective. It helps me see a bigger picture. It even seems to speed up the healing process. There is a saying that we will reap what we sow—maybe in our helping others to heal, we heal a part of ourselves as well, without even trying.

There are enough girls out there who are spiteful, jealous, angry, and back-stabbing. To put it bluntly, that's just wrong. We girls will face enough problems in this world without us causing grief for each other.

Look after your friends. Support each other. Ask how your friends are doing.

Then ask how they are *really* doing. Take the time to send them small notes or to leave them encouraging phone messages. It will mean the world to your friend if she's having a rough day.

If your friend is going through something and you're not sure what to do or say, just show up and hang out for a while. You can even tell your friend that you're uncomfortable because you don't know what to say, but you'd like to help. Your friend will be glad that you made the effort, trust me.

So take what you have learned about beauty, guys, and God, and pass it on to someone who could really use the encouragement. Don't forget about those who are looking up to you as a role model. Take the wisdom that you have learned and the strength that you have gained and pass it along to someone who is traveling through where you have already been.

Things I've Learned: Help someone else out along the way—help a sista out!

Confessions of a Non-Barbie

About the Author

Kinda resides in Tulsa, Oklahoma, and is an instructor at Oklahoma State University. She has taught classes ranging from Leadership to Organizational Behavior and has won multiple teaching awards.

Kinda serves as the worship leader at The Sanctuary Christian Worship Center in Chelsea, Oklahoma. She also works with organizations such as WINGS (Women Impacting the Nations by God's Spirit) Ministries, where she speaks to teen girls and directs a district-wide women's choir.

For more information, contact Kinda at:

Website: www.kindawilson.com 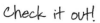 Check it out!

Email: info@kindawilson.com

Endnotes

Section: Being a Single Girl

[1]single. (n.d.). Dictionary.com Unabridged (v 1.1). Retrieved January 26, 2009, from Dictionary.com website: http://dictionary.reference.com/browse/single

[2]disease. (n.d.). The American Heritage® Dictionary of the English Language, Fourth Edition. Retrieved January 26, 2009, from Dictionary.com website: http://dictionary.reference.com/browse/disease

Section: Looking for a Date

[1]"Love is the Drug, Scientists Say." BBC News. 25 Nov 2003. 26 Jan 2009 <http://news.bbc.co.uk/2/hi/health/3236328.stm>

[2]Lieberman & Williams, K. "Does Rejection Hurt? An fMRI Study of Social Exclusion." *Science* 10 October 2003: Vol. 302. no. 5643, pp. 290 - 292.

Section: Dating

[1]faith. (n.d.). Dictionary.com Unabridged (v 1.1). Retrieved January 26, 2009, from Dictionary.com website: http://dictionary.reference.com/browse/faith

[2]fear. (n.d.). Dictionary.com Unabridged (v 1.1). Retrieved January 26, 2009, from Dictionary.com website: http://dictionary.reference.com/browse/fear

Section: Breakups - the Real Deal

[1]reject. (n.d.). The American Heritage® Dictionary of the English Language, Fourth Edition. Retrieved January 26, 2009, from Dictionary.com website: http://dictionary.reference.com/browse/reject

[2]catharsis. (n.d.). Dictionary.com Unabridged (v 1.1). Retrieved January 26, 2009, from Dictionary.com website: http://dictionary.reference.com/browse/catharsis

[3]catharsis. (n.d.). The American Heritage® Dictionary of the English Language, Fourth Edition. Retrieved January 26, 2009, from Dictionary.com website: http://dictionary.reference.com/browse/catharsis

[4]gangrene. (n.d.). Dictionary.com Unabridged (v 1.1). Retrieved May 12, 2009, from Dictionary.com website: http://dictionary1.classic.reference.com/browse/gangrene

[5]Greenfield, Ronald A. "Gangrene." eMedicine Health
12 April 2009< http://www.emedicinehealth.com/gangrene/article_em.htm>

[6]"Medical Encyclopedia - Gangrene." U.S. National Library of Medicine
11 September 2006<http://www.nlm.nih.gov/medlineplus/ency/article/007218.htm>

Section: Moving on...Eventually

[1]Millon, Theodore, Blaney, Paul, & Davis, Roger. (Ed.). (1999). Oxford Textbook of Psychopathology. New York, NY: Oxford University Press, Inc.

[2]"What are the Signs and Symptoms of Depression?" National Institute of Mental Health. Retrieved 25 May 2009 from <"http://www.nimh.nih.gov/health/publications/depression/what-are-the-signs-and-symptoms-of-depression.shtml>

[3]"The Three E's: Exercise, Endorphins and Euphoria." Mens Health
30 April 2009 <http://www.mens-total-fitness.com/endorphins.html>

[4]Scott, Elizabeth. "Music and Your Body: How Music Affects Us and Why Music Therapy Promotes Health" About.com Health and Disease. 1 November, 2007.

PRAYER OF SALVATION

God loves you—no matter who you are, no matter what your past. God loves you so much that He gave His one and only begotten Son for you. The Bible tells us that "...whoever believes in him shall not perish but have eternal life" (John 3:16 NIV). Jesus laid down His life and rose again so that we could spend eternity with Him in heaven and experience His absolute best on earth. If you would like to receive Jesus into your life, say the following prayer out loud and mean it from your heart.

Heavenly Father, I come to You admitting that I am a sinner. Right now, I choose to turn away from sin, and I ask You to cleanse me of all unrighteousness. I believe that Your Son, Jesus, died on the cross to take away my sins. I also believe that He rose again from the dead so that I might be forgiven of my sins and made righteous through faith in Him. I call upon the name of Jesus Christ to be the Savior and Lord of my life. Jesus, I choose to follow You and ask that You fill me with the power of the Holy Spirit. I declare that right now I am a child of God. I am free from sin and full of the righteousness of God. I am saved in Jesus' name. Amen.

If you prayed this prayer to receive Jesus Christ as your Savior for the first time, please contact us on the Web at:

www.harrisonhouse.com

to receive a free book.

Or you may write to us at:

Harrison House • P.O. Box 35035 • Tulsa, Oklahoma 74153

Fast. Easy.
Convenient.

For the latest Harrison House product information and author news, look no further than your computer. All the details on our powerful, life-changing products are just a click away. New releases, E-mail subscriptions, testimonies, monthly specials—find it all in one place. Visit harrisonhouse.com today!

harrisonhouse